When You Pray

Finbarr Lynch SJ

First published in 2012 by Messenger Publications

Messenger Publications,
37 Lower Leeson Street, Dublin 2
www.messenger.ie

Printed in Ireland

ISBN 978-1-872245-86-7

Designed by Messenger Publications Design Department
Typeset in Centaur

MESSENGER
PUBLICATIONS
JESUITS in IRELAND

This book had its beginnings in a series of ten-minute talks on prayer to assist retreatants at Manresa Retreat House, Dollymount, Dublin 3 during 2007, 2008 and 2009. Although designed originally to help retreatants, my hope is that these talks will have a wider application and, in their present form, be of considerable assistance to all who are seriously interested in personal prayer.

Contents

Chapter 1

Prayer is a Journey

Introduction

✤This book had its beginnings in a series of ten-minute talks on prayer to assist retreatants at Manresa Retreat House, Dollymount, Dublin 3 during 2007, 2008 and 2009. Although designed originally to help retreatants, my hope is that these talks will have a wider application and, in their present form, be of considerable assistance to all who are seriously interested in personal prayer. The heart of the book is in chapters four to twelve, drawn from directions to retreatants on how to pray during an eight-day retreat. To these I have added three introductory chapters: on prayer as journey, on images of God and on right desire in prayer. After chapter twelve, I have added five more chapters: on review of prayer, on guidance for the next time of prayer, on the Sign of the Cross as a prayer, and, after the concluding chapter, an appendix for retreatants to help them bring their retreat to a fruitful close. And finally, a summary of the steps of approach to prayer.

Prayer is Natural

✤I am inclined to believe that all people pray at some time. I recall the observation of the wife of a diplomat, who, tired of the shallow pleasantries and bland exchanges at diplomatic gatherings, decided to begin asking those she met what place prayer had in their lives: 'How do you pray?' To her pleasant surprise she discovered that all those she asked, from different cultures and religions, prayed and reached out to some higher power to ask for help or to express gratitude. Prayer seems to correspond to some need in all of us when we acknowledge to ourselves that we are not in complete control and that we are faced with a certain riddle about our own life, for life is indeed something of a puzzle. Prayer is natural.

Prayer is a dialogue

⚜ Many who build on this need, this inner urge, make time for daily prayer. Either we use prayers composed by others, such as the psalms from the Bible, or we talk in our own words about our needs and concerns in a one-sided conversation, trusting that we are being heard. If we persevere, we come to a point where we sense that there is more to prayer than the saying of prayers. Those of us whose only prayer is the saying of prayers are keeping a one-sided control of the relationship that prayer is meant to be; this obviously limits the relationship, and it limits the experience of the prayer, too. If I want to know that I am being heard, if I want to hear some echo from my prayers and learn what God is communicating to me, I will need to go beyond the formulas I use and discover how to listen, how to pick up the signals that are coming from this God who wants an active part in my praying. Such a development takes time, however, for prayer, like love, is a long journey and is learnt by doing.

Prayer is a journey

⚜ The long journey of growth in prayer has many stages of development. I remember a story which illustrates a well-developed stage in the journey.

A businessman, call him John, who took prayer seriously, came to me a few years ago to ask me if I would accompany him on his inner journey. I knew already that he had made the *Spiritual Exercises* of St Ignatius in their daily life form, an adventure of praying every day over the life, death and resurrection of Jesus during a long period of about nine months — and that prayer had by now put down roots in his daily life. He was a married man. He was amazingly successful in his business. During our first conversation, I asked him, "What is prayer like for you now?" He told me this story.

He recalled Pat Kenny's chat-show, entitled "Kenny Live". One morning, Pat Kenny was interviewing Yehudi Menuhin, the world-renowned virtuoso violinist. Kenny asked, "Mr Menuhin, is music good for your health?" Menuhin answered with warmth and some solemnity, "Music coordinates my life." John then said to me, "Prayer coordinates **my** life."

Menuhin's life revolved around music-playing, conducting, fostering the talent of gifted young players, and travelling the world. He served music; it was what gave meaning to all parts of his life; it determined his choices; and it brought out the best in him. He was committed heart and soul to music; it was a relationship for him. But in order to get the most out of his rare musical capacity, he had to be self-disciplined in his lifestyle.

John was a notable success in business, but here he was telling me that his business was not the centre of his life. Something else was; he called it prayer. By this he meant his personal relationship with Jesus of which prayer was an essential expression. He was committed heart and soul to Jesus. Just as Menuhin could not live or make sense of his life without music, so also my friend could not live or make sense of his life without the regular personal prayer in which he was meeting with the One who loved him. Time had to be found for it, for this relationship with Jesus was what gave meaning to everything else — his marriage, his business, his reaching out to others, his leisure times. Prayer was the special time and space where he met his Lord. There he found energy, there he felt at home, there he found depth, and there also he found guidance for his choices. This relationship drew him beyond self-interest and into self-donation. Prayer was coordinating his life.

Questions for reflection:

1) What coordinates my life? Is it my job, my role, my profession?"
2) What do I live for? Is there something in my life that is deep enough for me to give my heart to?
3) Do I want to find a central focus that will harmonise my life and bring out the best in me? What fear am I conscious of around this?
4) Would a growing relationship with the Lord expressed in personal prayer hold any attraction for me? Would it answer some yearning that I should listen to?
5) Do I want to learn more about personal prayer?

Chapter 2

God and I

Image of God

✢ There is a well-known passage in the Book of Job where God is portrayed as speaking from the heart of a storm. It is a rather fearsome image. "From the heart of the tempest the Lord gave Job his answer." (Job 38:1) The Lord is surrounded by a storm to impress upon Job that he is the Lord, the Almighty One, who instils fear and will brook no opposition. The Almighty One demands submission of Job who has dared contend with him: "Who is this, obscuring my intentions with his ignorant words?... Where were you when I laid the earth's foundations?" (38:2,4) And then, after a long portrayal of God as Creator of the universe, Job acknowledges abjectly that he has spoken out of turn; he says, "My words have been frivolous: what can I reply? I had better lay my hand over my mouth." (40:4) The Lord God is presented here as the Creator who is to be feared and obeyed, and held in great respect.

This reading from Job and the image of God that it presents puts me in mind of a topic that arises for us when we make a serious effort to pray. There are two related questions: the first is, "**Who is God for me?**", and the second is, "**Who am I for God?**" These two questions arise either **explicitly** or **implicitly** because our prayer time is a meeting with God. "Who is this God whom I am meeting? What is he like? What is my perception of him?" And "Who am I for God? What does he see in me? How is he regarding me?" There is a lifelong spiritual journey encompassed within these two broad questions, for I am always needing to grow in my perception of who **God** is for me, and I am also needing to see **myself** through God's eyes.

Who is God for me?

✢I am not speaking here about an intellectual and correct answer which may be learned from the catechism or from theology or spiritual books or even the Bible. Sound answers to the question, "Who is God?" may be part of my thinking about God; but it is quite possible that my thinking about God is quite different from the perception of God that is real for me and comes into play in my prayer and my life, the image of God that is operative for me. For there is a difference between "Who is God?" and "Who is God for me?" In prayer it is the operative image or perception of God that comes into play. During prayer, I approach God with my operative image of him. How near to the truth about God is it? Is it far away from how God wants to be seen by me?

Stages

It goes without saying that our image of God cannot help but fall short of who God really is, for the full truth about God is necessarily beyond the power of our limited minds to grasp. Nevertheless, it is also true that we can grow closer and closer to the truth about God, for God has revealed himself in scripture and wants to reveal himself to me in prayer. My perception of who God is **for me** goes through stages of development linked to my own development **as a person**. There is a certain match between now how I am in myself and how I am perceiving God in my life and my prayer.

Take, for example, a person preoccupied by law, rules and right behaviour in his or her life. Such a one is conscientious, conscious of duty, becoming self-disciplined, and is no longer dominated by mood or whim. This is a necessary and good stage of development. The Pharisees in the gospels were like this. They were good men, wanting to do what was God's will as they saw it. But their trouble was that they became stuck at this stage, fixated on the level of performance, whereas Jesus was inviting them to come deeper to the level of the heart, where they would pay attention to their motives for their actions. The person of law is focused on rules and observances and performance, and that is good but it is not a place at which to remain, **for there is more.** Such a person will tend to see God as Lawgiver, Judge, Accountant, someone who is watching with a critical eye and assessing. God may be seen as a demanding God and viewed with some fear. This was how Job was perceiving and experiencing God. God, as Creator, was portrayed as asserting his dominion. And Job was led to acknowledge that his questioning attitude was out of order. He humbled himself before his Creator.

Who am I for God?

✤ This Lord, who is my Creator, is asking of me not only obedience and humility; he is requesting of me not only a life lived by his commandments. My Creator is making an **offer** to me, inviting me into a personal, conscious relationship of love with himself. He wants me to awaken to the deep truth of what it means to be a creature, namely, that my Creator is loving me into existence and is doing this continuously. The Creator, who is portrayed as speaking correctively to Job from the storm, is loving me into existence. I exist because God wants me to exist; he loves me, and so I exist. I am attractive in God's eyes; I am 'precious' to him. (Is 43:4)

To accept this truth is a big shift in my perception of **who I am**, and in my image of **who God is**. A new level of relationship with God comes into view. But there is more.

There is more

⊕This God wants **my heart.** As my Creator, God is giving me **his heart** already by loving me without reserve. But there is more. Over the long history of salvation God has revealed more of his desire towards us by arriving at the extraordinary point of giving us his Son, giving me his Son so that I can be not only a loved creature but an adopted son or daughter, sharing in the Sonship of Jesus, sharing in the inner life of the Three Persons. It takes time and God's grace to become able to hear this in such a way that it is real for me and comes into play in my prayer and my life. God can only love me: I am his heart's delight. He wants me to hear this in my heart, to hear it in an **operative** way. Personal prayer is a privileged place in which to hear it. This, it seems to me, is a lifelong spiritual journey.

Questions for reflection:

1) Who is God for me? Do I notice this coming into play in how I pray?

2) Is my perception of who God is changing lately? Has it gone through stages over the years?

3) In my service of God, am I more focused on performance and duty, and less focused on the motivations going on in my heart? Why do I do what I do?

4) Do I desire to taste God's love for me? Will I ask for this?

Chapter 3

Desiring God

To find or to be found?

✠People come to prayer in order to *find* Jesus and be with him. You have put time aside from the other things you could be doing and, instead, are devoting it to being with Jesus. You do this because you treasure that relationship of faith in which you meet Jesus and grow in his friendship. You want to *find* him; but when you remember that God is seeking us more than we him, it would be better to have it in your mind that you have come in order *to be found* by Jesus. Jesus is hungering and thirsting for relationship with us, and is *active* during our time of prayer. This way of thinking fits in well with the meaning of the Incarnation, by which God chose to be *one of us* in order to bring us close; he is still seeking us.

What kind of desire

✠What is your desire for Jesus like? What do you want from him? Is your desire self-centred? We might learn something in this regard from what happened in John 6: 22-29. Jesus had miraculously fed the 5,000. The next day they came looking for Jesus. They were very eager in their desire for him. They searched and eventually found him at Capernaum. We can learn something for ourselves from what happened next.

On the surface

When the people found Jesus, they asked him a superficial question, "Rabbi, *when* did you come here?" Jesus hears the shallowness of that enquiry. He sees that they have not perceived the underlying meaning of what he had done for them: they have seen only a *wondrous* deed and *free* bread.

Jesus goes straight to the point. He challenges them: "You are looking for me because you had all the bread you wanted to eat." (6:26) They wanted Jesus, and that seemed good on the surface, but they were being *self-centred* in their quest and *shallow* in their perception of him; and in addition, we know that their dreams of a *political Messiah* had been awakened, for, as John tells us, "they (had) intended to come and make him king by force." (6:15) Their political ambitions, and also their self-centredness were **blinding** them from seeing and desiring Jesus as he wanted to be seen and desired. They wanted free gifts of a physical kind; they wanted to satisfy a hunger that was only of the body; they wanted to get but not to give. The freedom they wanted was political but not the freedom of the heart that Jesus was offering. They were on the surface of themselves.

A shallow approach

It is possible in daily personal prayer, or even during a retreat, to be wanting Jesus in a **shallow** and **self-centred** way. This can be happening in many different ways without our realising it. I could, for instance, be seeking Jesus in order to find pleasant feelings; I could, in my praying, be wanting the pleasant consolations of God instead of wanting the God of consolations; I could be in prayer or on retreat on my own terms, not God's. I could be like those men and women in **John 6** whose focus was mainly on the gift of bread.

It is possible to stay **superficial** in my prayer and decline the invitation to come deeper. I can do this, for instance, by holding **control** over my way of praying: being rigid about it, wanting to feel secure through it, instead of letting the Lord teach me how he wants me to be in his presence now;

for prayer goes through changes according as we grow in our relationship with him. I can stay superficial by staying in my **head** during prayer, thinking interesting thoughts but not meeting the Lord. I can stay superficial, also, by being too **afraid** to come down to the level of my heart where I am invited to trust and to let myself be loved without deserving it, and to hear the Lord's desire for me. It is even possible to stay superficial by clinging to my **anxieties** and to my anger and to my memories of hurt. I can stay superficial by keeping the main focus on **myself**.

Another kind of hunger

✛ Jesus has just said to those superficial seekers in John 6, "You are looking for me, not because you have seen the signs, but because you had all the bread you wanted to eat." (6:26) Then he focuses his challenge when he goes on to say, "Do not work for food that cannot last." (6:27) Why does he say this? What is he pointing to? He is telling them that there is **another** kind of food and **another** kind of hunger. The way of the **world-without-God** is to stay on the surface of myself; this is the way of possessions and prestige and power and competitiveness. But the way of Jesus is to come deeper, down to the level of heart and spirit. There is a space down there in each of us that only God can fill. In that deep space, we hunger. During prayer, we let that hunger become conscious. The food that matches this deep hunger is relationship with Jesus in faith. Jesus is offering this relationship; he wants us to have it. This is the other kind of "bread". A faith relationship with him is what Jesus means by "bread" when he calls himself "the bread of life" in the first part of the discourse in John 6. He says to them, and now also to us, "**Work** for the kind of food the Son of Man is offering you". (6:27)

What is this **work**? It is to believe, to enter a relationship of faith: "This is carrying out God's work: you must believe in the one he has sent." (6:29) What is Jesus **offering**? Himself, conscious relationship with himself. It is as if he is saying to each of us, "Believe, come into the circle of relationship and find a developing relationship with me. It will satisfy your deepest hunger. You are made for this. It is worth working at."

During personal prayer we cross over to the other side, not of the Lake of Galilee, but of ourselves. We reach down to our authentic self. We let our deepest hunger become conscious; we let it lead us to Jesus. He wants to give us himself in deep friendship.

Questions for reflection:

1) What are you looking for when you pray?
2) How much do you believe that Jesus is seeking you out?
3) Do you work too hard in your personal prayer?
4) Are you aware of a tendency to stay on the surface during prayer?
5) Will you allow Jesus to come to you on his terms?

Come, Holy Spirit, Spirit of Love, Spirit of discipline.
In the Silence,
  COME to us and bring us your PEACE;
  REST in us that we may be tranquil and still.
In the Silence,
  SPEAK to us as each heart needs to hear;
  REVEAL to us things hidden and things longed for.
In the Silence,
  REJOICE in us that we may praise and be glad;
  PRAY in us that we may be at one with You and with
  each other.
In the Silence,
  REFRESH and RENEW us from your LIVING
  SPRINGS OF WATER.
Holy Spirit, DWELL in us that Your LIGHT may shine
  through us,
and that in our heart YOU may find
Your homeliest home and endless dwelling. Amen.

Chapter 4
God At Work

✟ These short reflections are not intended for giving you points or ideas to pray on. They are about how to approach prayer; they focus on the attitudes or dispositions that may help you in your prayer. It is likely that these reflections will be reminding you of what you already know, but this is no harm, for we hear things differently according as we change and grow in ourselves.

How do you see time dedicated to prayer?

✠ I invite you to begin by reflecting on how you see the time you dedicate to prayer. What is your image or metaphor for it? The image that says it for you will help you to cooperate with the Holy Spirit who is at work in you.

The Holy Spirit will be at work in you when you pray, and in some way you will not be at work. This puts me in mind of an old Latin tag for an extended time of prayer called a retreat, namely, "vacatio Deo": it means idleness for God, emptiness before God, a vacation or holiday with God. The time you spend in prayer is time put beyond usefulness to yourself. Prayer is not useful: it is something of a different order. In order to set aside time for personal prayer you come away from your usual preoccupations and concerns and achievements so as to be in some respect empty, idle, available to God. What you bring to prayer is just yourself and your time and your desire to be with God: you come with your availability. If you, for your part, are going to be less busy, and even idle, this would suggest that God is the main ACTOR in your prayer. The main AGENT in prayer is God, so what happens in prayer is God's AGENDA; God wants to be the busy one.

The setting

✠ If this busy God is to succeed in what he wants to do for us, he needs us to be in something of a wilderness, where nothing much is happening. In Hosea 2:14, God says to his people Israel,

> *"Therefore, I will now **allure** her,*
> *And bring her into the **wilderness**,*
> *And speak to her **heart**."*

Your dedicated time for prayer is something of a

wilderness already, for you have turned off your mobile phone and radio and TV. You have drawn back from the customary noise and chatter that keeps you on the surface of yourself. God wants to draw you deep, into your heart. If you cooperate with God at work within you, you can have those **wilderness** conditions that heighten your sensitivity to God's word; and you will be **allured** by God's attractiveness, and God will speak to your **heart**. Create something of a solitude around yourself when you pray so as to be truly alone with God.

The story of Moses in **Exodus, chapter 3** picks up on these three points: the **wilderness**, the **allurement**, and the **revelation**. I will reflect on each of these in turn.

The wilderness: "I will bring her into the wilderness".

Moses has led the flock he was minding farther into the wilderness; we are told that he "led his flock to the far side of the wilderness, and came to HOREB, the mountain of God" (3:1) The wilderness is a land not cultivated, but it has grass enough for the sheep to graze upon, and many beautiful flowers, but also some wild animals. It is far away from thoroughfares and trade routes. There are few people around, or even none. And now Moses is going further away from home and from people, and already finds himself surrounded by a great quiet. All he has to do is keep his sheep together and be on the watch against predators. He is very much alone, and is undistracted. He is ideally placed now for God to catch his attention.

You, by drawing aside for personal prayer, are also entering a **wilderness**. By your regular commitment to prayer, you enter further into this wilderness in hope of coming to the **mountain** of God. This mountain of God is deep within you, in your **heart**. This wilderness, too, is within you: you create it for yourself by coming away from your preoccupations and from people and from exterior noise. You create wilderness conditions for yourself so that you can find a certain sense of solitude and become able to notice God's delicate approach to your heart. You slow down inside yourself.

The allurement: "I will now allure her."

Moses has slowed down, too, and has time now to notice his surroundings better. He notices a bush blazing with fire. Then he observes that it is not being burned up. If he was hurrying along, intent on getting from A to B, he might not have been able to notice this strange happening. This bush is alive with flame. He in intrigued, so he moves closer in order to focus better. He gives it all his attention. Here God is **captivating** Moses.

You, too, can slow down during your chosen time of prayer, and so can become better able to notice how attractive a word or phrase in a scripture passage has become. Something that you have passed over many times before is now drawing you with a mysterious attraction. It has lit up for you. If you are free enough of your own agenda, you will linger here, like Moses did, and let it captivate you; you will engage with the attraction and find connectedness with the Lord; you will linger here until you are satisfied.

The revelation: "I will speak to her heart."

Moses goes forward to look at this bush. He is in a state of wonderment. This opens him to mystery. God, who is the Mysterious One, reveals that he is present here, alive like that flame. He does this by addressing Moses by name, from the bush. "God called to him out of the bush, 'Moses, Moses'. (3:4) Moses now feels recognised by Someone.

Then, two more things happen. Firstly, he is instructed to be reverent, for this is "holy ground". Secondly, the

Speaker reveals, not only the fact that he is present here, but who he is: "I am the God of your ancestors, the God of Abraham, the God of Isaac, and the God of Jacob." (3:6) The effect on Moses is fear and awe: "Moses hid his face, because he was afraid to look at God. (3:6)

We note that the bush and its flame were outside Moses, but the intimate and awesome meeting with God was taking place **inside** Moses: God was speaking to his heart.

Something like this can happen in you when a word or a phrase lights up. It becomes a "burning bush", just for you, in this moment. The attraction you are experiencing opens you to mystery, and allows God to reach into you. This attraction is God at work, revealing himself, awakening you to his active presence inside you, alive like the flame in the bush. This flame will not consume you or harm you. It is God speaking to your heart. As it was with Moses, God asks you, too, to be reverent here, for you are meeting God. You will linger here, out of reverence. Moses recognised the God of his ancestors. You, as a Christian, will recognise that the One now meeting you here in your prayer is the Risen Christ, drawing you and speaking to your heart.

Your personal prayer, in the wilderness space that you create for yourself, is about letting Christ capture your attention and tell you he is alive in your heart, like that flame in the bush, and reveal his love to you. Christ is active in your prayer. Your wilderness is a graced place.

Concluding Prayer

> *TAKE, Lord, the little that I offer, the tiny one I am;*
> *and GIVE me the much that I hope for, the all that is you.*
> *Amen.*

O Lord my God,
Teach my heart where and how to seek you,
  where and how to find you.
O Lord, you are my God and you are my Lord,
  and I have never seen you. You have made me and
  re-made me, and you have bestowed on me all the
  good things I possess, and still I do not know you...
Teach me to seek you, and as I seek you show yourself to
me,
  for I cannot seek you unless you teach me how,
  nor will I ever find you unless you show yourself to me.
Let me seek you by desiring you, let me desire you by
  seeking you.
Let me find you by loving you, let me love you when I find
  you.

(St Anselm of Canterbury)

Chapter 5

Approaching Prayer

✤In the previous chapter, I invited you to reflect in a broad way on how you see the time dedicated to prayer. I spoke of it as a time of **availability** to God who wants to be the main AGENT in personal prayer. God needs us to be in something of a **wilderness** here, undistracted, quiet, available, and sensitive to God's "tiny whispering voice." **(1 Kings 19:12)** I connected **Hosea 2:14** with the experience of Moses recounted in **Exodus 3:1-6**, and I reflected on the **wilderness**, the **allurement** of the burning bush, and on God **revealing** himself to Moses' heart.

Personal prayer can also be seen as a journey into the unknown, an adventure, as a mystery tour, and for this we can see ourselves invited into an attitude of TRUST.

Another metaphor for the prolonged meeting with God in personal prayer is to see God as the **Gracious Host** who welcomes us, listens to us, feeds our deepest hunger with himself, and tells us his love and his will for us. In **Revelation 3:20**, we hear his desire to share a meal with us. He says, "Listen! I am standing at the door, knocking; if you hear my voice and open the door, I will come in to you and eat with you, and you with me." He says he is waiting; will I open to him? What will he notice? Where will his gaze be? What exchange does he want? What am I hungry for?

Experience of prayer

✠ In this chapter, I want to take a closer look at prayer itself, at what happens during the experience of prayer. How do you see your prayer? What is your image of prayer? You may be sure that you do have a way of perceiving your prayer, and it is either helping you or hindering you. Do you long for prayer? Or is it a time that you tend to avoid? Is it a time that goes sweetly for you, or a time that feels like watering a dry stick? Is it a duty for you; or is it a time when you come back to yourself and feel gathered together again? Is prayer something done by you from start to finish; or is it something done to you, received by you? Or is it a prayer of faith, like being in a cinema without knowing where the screen is, and so you have no focus?

Core longing for God

✠ There are levels in us. In our deepest centre, we are longing for prayer, longing for communion with God; but at our surface level, we feel a certain resistance to prayer, and we have to go against an ego-self level in order to get through to the deeper level where we are being drawn to prayer. It is rather like going for a swim in Irish sea-water – difficult to begin with, but good when you are in it. In prayer, we enter a space of self-transcendence. The Holy Spirit within us is drawing us down to this space. The Spirit is in our core, calling out, "Abba, Father," and giving us the taste of our true self as a daughter or a son of God. But on the surface, we may feel little attraction towards prayer when we start to pray.

Does your image of prayer help you to overcome the surface resistance and to pay attention to your core longing for God?

Prayer is a meeting

✢My suggestion for you is that you look upon prayer as a MEETING. Someone important is waiting for you, and you stop whatever else you are doing in order to allow a meeting to happen. Someone who really loves you is looking at you, and now you enter that gaze of love. You come inside the field of an enormous radiation of real love, and you advert to it in prayer, and you receive.

THE FIRST STEP ~ Presence to myself

✢To prepare myself for the meeting that prayer is, the very **first** thing to do is to come in touch with myself. We arrive at our prayer time carrying a jumble inside ourselves-feelings and reactions of all sorts. Much of this we keep out of sight from ourselves. We may be afraid of some of it. But, if our prayer is to be **real**, we must try to be real with ourselves as much as we can. So I begin by asking myself, "What has been happening to me? How am I now? Can I be real with myself?"

Say I meet with a close friend after hearing disappointing

or upsetting news, and this friend, who knows me well, asks me, "How are you?"; if I, then, try to deflect the attention from myself by saying, "I'm fine. How are you?", my friend, who knows me well, is sure to sense that I am not in good form. A real interaction can't happen between us until I admit to how I **really** am. Then, the usual good flow between us will happen, and we can be intimate.

It is the same with my meeting with God. Unless I am **in touch** with myself as best I can, I will not have a good flow of connectedness with God. This is so because I will be hiding part of **me** from myself, and trying to hide it from God, also. So my **first step** for entering prayer will be to touch base with myself: "How am I?"

Feelings
What will I discover? The feelings I find may be bright or dark, welcome or unwelcome. I don't call them good or bad, for my feelings are **pre-moral**; they have a reason to be there; and they are even right to be there, in view of my experience and my history; so I give them permission by **acknowledging** them. The moral question enters the scene when I choose how I will act on them, but here I simply acknowledge them. The Psalms, which are inspired prayers, are full of a whole range of feelings, and these are turned into **stepping-stones** towards God.

Approaching the next step
✦Having got in touch with how I am feeling, I am ready now to take the **next step**. I lift my eyes off myself and look towards the One who is waiting to interact with me. I may bring my feelings to him, or I may let go of them by leaving them in his care. I am ready now to look away from myself and to approach God. This is a **transition** and it takes time.

Transition

For making this transition, I may take on board the suggestion of St Ignatius. He suggests that I approach prayer as though I were standing outside the sacred room of prayer; I put my hand on the door-knob, and I pause. I ask myself two questions: "Where am I going, and for what purpose?" His own words are:

"Before entering into prayer I will allow the spirit to rest a little, by sitting down or strolling about, as seems best to me, while considering where I am going and for what purpose." (*Spiritual Exercises* 239 and 131)

I am not to rush into prayer: it is a sacred meeting, so I **pause** before it.

"Where am I going?" Into a sacred space, holy ground, the place where God dwells. And where is that place? It is in my heart, in my innermost centre. Here I am unique; no one else is like me. I want to come home to myself.

"And for what purpose?" To interact with this Lord, to let the Lord radiate his love upon me; to let the Lord enlighten me; to let the Lord come close to me. I want to let him have my heart. Note that my purpose is expressed in a receptive way: I want to allow the Lord; the initiative is his.

My hand is still on the door-knob; I am outside the sacred space. What do I do next? I **open** the door, and there I find the Lord **looking** at me. **What kind of a look is this?**

Ignatius suggests: "I will consider how God our Lord is **looking** at me." (*Spiritual Exercises* 75) It is the Risen Jesus. What is his gaze saying to me? The meeting has begun.

Concluding prayer

> *TAKE, Lord, the little that I offer, the tiny one I am;*
> *and GIVE me the much that I hope for, the all that is you. Amen.*

O Lord Jesus Christ,
who are the Way, the Truth and the Life,
we pray you permit us not
to stray from you who are the Way,
nor to distrust in you who are the Truth,
nor to rest in any other thing than you who are the Life.
Teach us by your Holy Spirit
what to do,
what to believe,
and wherein to take our rest   Amen
                    (A prayer of Desiderius Erasmus)

Chapter 6

Meeting God's Gaze

✢In the previous chapter, I asked you to consider how you see your personal prayer, whether you experience it as drawing you or as hard to face into, whether it is like a duty for you or is a healing experience where you come home to yourself, whether it is something you work at or you receive. I spoke of our core longing for God in our deepest centre, for we are made for God; but there is also a certain resistance to prayer at the surface level of ourselves. Then I proposed that you would see prayer as a MEETING with Someone who is waiting for you. To prepare myself for a real meeting with a friend, I come in touch with myself as I am, without my usual masks, as if I were the Tax Collector in the parable told by Jesus in **Luke 18**. I accept my dark or bright feelings. Then I focus towards the meeting that is prayer. I pause, and I consider where

I am going, and why. My hand is still on the door-knob outside the sacred room.

THE SECOND STEP ~ Presence to God

✠ What do I do next? I open the door, I enter the sacred space inside me, and there I find God our Lord looking at me. Who is this? It is the Risen Jesus, now present everywhere and sustaining the whole universe in existence, for he is "the Word through whom all things were made." (John 1:3) Here he is, personally present to me. This Mysterious One is totally aware of me, for he is loving me into existence and holding me in existence; he is looking at me now in prayer. I bow interiorly in my heart. My puny mind cannot grasp all this.

St Ignatius suggests, as I have already said: "I will consider how God our Lord is looking at me." (*Sp Ex* 75) How is the Risen Jesus looking at me? My answer will be as rich as my insight into who the Risen Jesus is in relation to me, but for the present let us stay with the suggestion of St Teresa of Avila:

> *Imagine you see Jesus standing before you.*
> *He is looking at you.*
> **Notice** *him looking at you.*
> *Notice him looking at you* **lovingly** *and* **humbly***.*
>
> (*Quoted in A. de Mello:* Sadhana *p. 113*)

I look at him looking at me. He is looking at me lovingly: he loves me now, just as I am. He is looking at me humbly: he became a servant and died willingly the death of a slave out of love for me. Can I **accept** this humble and loving look? Or will I turn away in self-disapproval? Do I realise yet how much I mean to him? He has given his life for me; he is now looking for a conscious and intimate relationship with me. I realise that no one is worthy of this: it is an **unearned** gift. But do I want this gift? Can I accept an unearned gift? It is hard for us, who are adults, to accept something that we have not earned.

Friendship

Prayer is a MEETING with this Jesus who is looking at me now and offering me the gift of his friendship. For a friendship to go well, the action needs to be shared. I have a part to play, but Jesus also has a part to play. Some of the prayer-time, therefore, has to be a listening on my part, a receiving, letting the Lord affect me – for he is active during prayer – and learning how to respond to his initiatives. Prayer is like a dance, in which God has the part played by the male partner but is leading me by signals that happen inside me and teaching me how to interact with him.

Learning how to pray

I need to be taught how to pray. Indeed, I am always learning how to be during prayer, for prayer is a gift given anew each time, and God is always greater and drawing me on. It is God himself who wants this intimacy with me. I don't know how to engage with One so different from me and so great. Close friends take time to learn the language of intimacy: they discover it together when they interact. But this close friend in my prayer time is Jesus the Lord. How can I know the language of intimate prayer except the Lord himself teaches me while I pray? I need to be taught to pray, so I ask.

THE THIRD STEP ~ Getting my focus right

✤The next step is to ask for the grace to have my focus right. This is what St Ignatius recommends in the *Spiritual Exercises*, and he calls it **The Preparatory Prayer**. I ask for the grace that all that I do and all that happens in me during my day, and especially now during this prayer time, be **directed purely to God's service and praise.** His own words are: "The preparatory prayer is to ask God our Lord for grace that all my intentions, actions and operations may be directed purely to the service and praise of his Divine Majesty." (*Sp Ex* 46). "Intentions, actions and operations": taken together, these three words mean "all my physical and mental efforts during this prayer period." (George Ganss S.J., translation and commentary, p.155) "The overall sense is clear: I am asking to approach through grace ever more closely to the ideal of a life totally dedicated to the service and praise of God." (Michael Ivens, S.J., *Understanding the Spiritual Exercises*, p. 47) This prayer for the grace of a right focus was very important to Ignatius.

Our Motives

I think it is fair to say that our motivation is usually mixed. We are full of self-interest. We need a Saviour to rescue us from ourselves. It may be rare for us to do something with pure, unmixed motivation. For this reason, I am in danger of entering upon prayer self-centredly, and spoiling the dance; I am likely to want the consolations of God instead of the God of consolations. My focus in prayer could be more on myself than on God. With this in mind, I ask earnestly for the grace that the **mixture** in my heart of "for-me" and "for-God" be better balanced, so that I can **put God first.** I want to be enabled by grace to say, "I am here for You: it is You I want." So I ask, "Give me the grace for this."

True to my being

I know that I want consolation. And God, for his part, does want to give me consolation. But this God, who loves me, will be teaching me by experience that consolation will come to me as an **overflow** of my wanting God more than myself. Why does it happen like this? It is because in my being I am made for God: this is the truth of who I am. So, when I ask for the grace of a right focus in prayer, to be there for God's service and praise, I am actually asking for the grace to be **true to my being**.

Whatever God gives

When I ask to get my focus right, something else will happen: I make myself **free** to accept whatever way the prayer will go. I tell myself, implicitly, that I am not here for a pleasant experience. What I want is that God be served and praised. A dry experience will be okay for me: for it is **God** I want.

Concluding Prayer

> *TAKE, Lord, the little that I offer, the tiny one I am;*
> *And GIVE me the much that I hope for, the all that is you,*
> *Amen.*

Do you wish to know the Lord's meaning in this thing?
*Know it well, **love was his meaning**.*
Who reveals it to you? **Love.**
What did he reveal to you? **Love.**
Why does he reveal it to you? **For love.**
Remain in this, and you will know more of the same.
But you will never know different, without end.

*So I was taught that **love is our Lord's meaning**.*
And I saw very certainly in this and in everything
that before God made us he loved us,
which love never abated and never will be.
And in this love he has done all his works,
and in this love he has made all things profitable to us,
and in this love our life is everlasting.
In our creation we had beginning,
but the love in which he created us was in him without
  beginning.
In this love we have our beginning.
        (Julian of Norwich *Showings* (Long text) Ch. 86)

Chapter 7

My Image of God and How God Regards Me

⚜In the previous chapter, I spoke about opening the door into the sacred space of prayer inside me. There I have met the gaze of the Lord. It is the Risen Jesus. I have accepted his loving and humble look. Knowing my need to be taught how to pray, I have asked for the grace to have my focus right, so that, in this meeting with God, I will be here more for God than for myself. I am not looking primarily for an experience that is pleasing to me: it is God I want, and to serve and praise him. I will accept whatever experience of prayer I am given.

Entering God's gaze

✦St Ignatius, in #75 of the *Spiritual Exercises*, suggests an approach to prayer that we have already partially explored: "I will consider how God our Lord is looking at me, and **other such thoughts.** Then I will make a genuflexion or some other act of humility." These three words, "other such thoughts," invite us into a wealth of reflection on our image of God. I want to open up some of this richness. It is an exploration of how God is towards us and who God is **for us.**

Ignatius' question is: **How is God our Lord looking at me?** I divide this question into two parts:
i) Who is this God?
ii) And what does he see when he is looking at us?

A. *i)* **Who is this God?**

God is the **Creator,** the ultimate source from whom everything is coming, and on whom everything depends, second by second. God is the MYSTERY enfolding our existence. God is **vast,** greater than the universe. At the same time, God is the most **intimate** one, dwelling within every atom anywhere. God is dwelling in every molecule of my body, and is inside my every thought and desire: no part of me is outside his presence or unknown to him. There is sheer mystery here, beyond my comprehension. God is so vast and yet so intimate: no image or metaphor is adequate to represent God. He called himself "I AM" when Moses asked to know his name in Exodus 3:14. The Psalmist in his prayer says: "O where can I go from your spirit, or where can I flee from your face?" (Ps. 139:7) Our Creator's awareness is all inclusive.

(ii) What does God see when he is looking at me?

As CREATOR, God sees his creature. To be a creature is to be receiving my whole being from my Creator. This is a continuous happening: I am coming from God's creative hand every second of my existence without interruption.

I am a bundle of gifts: everything I have and am is gift from Another, being poured out from God into me. He is sharing with me something of his own fullness. I might bring to mind the very many gifts that are mine: bodily gifts; intelligence; human will; talents of various kinds; particular skills, and the spiritual gifts of faith, hope and love which are part of my conscious relationship with God. All these gifts constitute who I am and are entrusted to me for my ongoing relationship with God.

A gift, as we know, spells **love**. I am being **loved into existence** without interruption. I exist because God wants me, because God is desiring me and always loving me. God, my Creator, is perfectly aware of me; he is looking at me all of the time. **What is his look saying?**

As my Creator, God, looking at me, is saying: "From all eternity I thought of you and wanted you; you are my delight; I love you."

When did God my Creator start saying this to me? God started saying his love to me as soon as I was just a fertilised ovum. And God has continued to say this all through my development, and is saying it now at this very moment. Whether I respond or not to this look of love, God keeps saying this love all the time, every single second. This love holds me in existence; this love is the whole cause of my existence. When I am approaching prayer, it is this gaze of love from God my Creator that I make myself aware of. I can grow in my awareness, and I can also grow in my response to his love.

B. *i)* Who is this God who is looking at me?

My Creator God is also my **FATHER**, for I have been baptised into the intimate life of the Trinity: I have a space there. I am sharing now in the space of the Sonship of Jesus. I have been chosen for this unearned dignity. The Father wants this for me.

ii) What does God my Father see when he is looking at me?

As FATHER, God, looking at me, sees his son or his daughter, his son or daughter whom he loves utterly. His look is saying, "You are mine." His gaze is saying, "I delight in you; I see my own features in you." He is saying to me now what he revealed he is saying from eternity to his Son, now incarnate, while Jesus was in prayer after the baptism by John, "You are my Son, whom I love: in you I delight" (Lk 3:22) I have been brought inside this radiation of approval and love, all unearned. This gaze is like sunshine: can I accept it? Can I rest under it and bask in it, enabled of course by the Holy Spirit? Or do I run back into disapproval of myself, feeling threatened by such acceptance of me as I am? What is preventing me?

The Father's gaze is also saying: I want a relationship of mutual love with you; I want you to share as fully as you can in my Son's space near me; I want you to know him and me intimately; I want you to experience our presence inside you; I want you to know how much you mean to us."

C. *i)* Who is this God who is looking at me?

This God, whom I meet in prayer, is also JESUS, the Incarnate Word, through whom the universe is being sustained in existence; he is now risen from the dead, and is present everywhere. He is mysteriously present, supporting me and the whole universe. He is my **Saviour**, my **Brother**, my **Lover**, and my **Leader**.

ii) And what does Jesus my Lord see when he is looking at me?

As my **Saviour**, he sees in me someone for whom he became a human being, someone for whom he gave his life.

His gaze is saying, "I want you to know how precious you are to me; I love you for yourself, just as you are, and I will bring you to where you really want to be: I took on your humanity and all its trouble so that you could receive a share in my divinity and all its happiness: I came to be with you so that you could be with me, and forever; I have given your evil a dead-end on my Cross; your sins are forgiven."

As my **Brother**, Jesus sees in me someone like himself, someone for whom he has unbounded compassion.

His gaze is saying: "I know what it is like to be a human being like you; I have stood in your shoes; I know your experience, the pain, the struggle, the confusion; my heart goes out to out; I will not let go of you."

As my **Lover**, Jesus sees in me someone he delights in and longs to be with, someone desirable whom he longs to communicate with and listen to, someone he can't do without.

His gaze is saying: "I am the One who completes you; you were made for friendship with me; I am your other half; I want union with you; I have paid the price for this; come, let us be together, deeply."

As my **Leader**, Jesus sees in me someone he needs for his

mission to the world, someone with gifts for this work, someone he is calling to work alongside him.

His gaze is also saying: "I still have work to do for my Father, and for this I need you; come, take up your cross every day for my sake, and follow me; let us work together for the salvation of humankind."

How am I to respond to the Lord's gaze?

✤ The **first response** must surely be to **receive** the Lord's gaze and his meaning. If I am able to rest for a while in that, this is prayer already. It is a mutual presence, it is a moment of intimacy. It is already a gesture of great respect to let oneself be looked at by someone so special.

The **second response** might be to do as St Ignatius suggests: "Then I will make a genuflexion or some other act of humility."

I am called to **respond** to this vast MYSTERY, this intimate CLOSENESS, this FATHER, this RISEN LORD

✤ with a genuflexion, at least interiorly, an inner act of reverence, for it is this Almighty One who is presenting himself to me;

✤ with humility, because I know my place. Of myself I am nothing, but to him I am so precious, for he has made me so. What he loves in me is what he has placed in me. I am NOTHING, and yet to him I am EVERYTHING.

A practical note

During prayer itself, it is unlikely that I can be conscious of all this material; I may be aware of just a small flavour of it for a while, or even consciously aware of none of it, and this would be quite in order. It is enough if it is in the **background**, shaping my **attitude** as I approach prayer, and opening me to this God who delights in me.

Other depths of Jesus can yield reflections on how he is regarding us when we meet him in prayer, e.g. Jesus as Teacher, as Lord, as Friend, as Healer, as Revealer, as Eucharist.

Concluding Prayer:

God of the universe, we worship you as Lord.
God, ever close to us, we rejoice to call you Father.
From this world's uncertainty we look to your covenant.
Keep us one in your peace, secure in your love.
We ask this through Christ our Lord. Amen.
                              (12th Sunday in Ordinary Time)

Lord, teach me to be generous,
Teach me to serve you as you deserve;
to give and not to count the cost;
to fight and not to heed the wounds;
to toil and not to seek for rest;
to labour and not to ask reward,
save that of knowing that I am doing your will.
Amen.
(accredited to St Ignatius Loyola)

Chapter 8

Jesus On Prayer

✤ In the previous chapter, I spoke about opening the door into the sacred space of prayer inside me. There I have met the gaze of the Lord. It is the Risen Jesus. I have accepted his loving and humble look. Knowing that I need to be taught how to pray, I have asked for the grace to have my focus right, so that, in this meeting with God, I will be here more for God than for myself. I am not looking primarily for an experience that is pleasing to me: it is God I want, and to serve and praise him. I will accept whatever experience of prayer I am given.

Jesus' approach to prayer

✤ St Ignatius seems to speak of pausing **outside** a sacred room, and then entering. In this chapter, I want to reflect on a different metaphor for entering prayer.

Jesus, in **Matthew 6:6**, speaks of **entering** a room,

shutting the door and then finding my Father waiting there for me.

> "But when you pray
> go into **your room**
> and shut the **door**
> and pray to **your Father** who is in secret.
> And your Father who sees in secret
> will **reward** you"

I seem to hear Jesus speaking here about his own experience of prayer and wanting to draw me into it. I note that the pronoun 'you' is in the singular in this verse: he is addressing me. I pick out the headings here: **your room...the door...your Father...the reward**. I want to comment upon these, one by one.

Your room: "go into your room." The room is **my heart**, my innermost self, the real me, where I am unique. I could picture myself going down by an inner lift to as deep a level inside myself as is accessible to me at present. I draw back into quietness, I gather myself together, and I descend.

The door: "and shut the door." Prayer is a meeting in the **present moment**; intimacy is in the present moment. So I shut the door on the **past** and on the **future** so as to be fully in the **present**. This step is a **transition**, so it is likely to require time. During prayer, I may have to search for the attitude towards something in my past or something in my future that will allow me to be in the present. It may be acceptance of pain regarding my **past**, or an attitude of trust in God in regard to the **future**.

Your Father: "and pray to your Father." I have shut the door. I am alone. There are no observers here. And now I find "my Father" waiting for me. I can be real here, without masks, for I am accepted already. Notice that Jesus says in the text, "your Father", not "the Father": "pray to **your** Father who is in secret". The word 'your' is in the singular here. If, then, this One who is waiting for me at my prayer time is "**my** Father", who then am I? I am a daughter or a son; and this is home. Prayer is about coming **home** to myself and to my Father. I could linger here over this realisation. My Father is welcoming me, his daughter, his son. He is saying now what he began to say at my baptism and ever since: "You are my daughter, my son, whom I love; in you I delight." **(Luke 3:22)** How will I respond? Will I stay for a while under his gaze? Let him delight in me? Adore my Lord? Or is it too much for me?

The reward: "And your Father will reward you". What might the reward be? What will my Father give to me? My suggestion is that the reward will be the **experience** of being at home in prayer, of knowing myself as a daughter or a son, of finding myself welcomed and accepted and forgiven and loved. The reward, I think, is in the **experience of meeting.**

Jesus' own praying

✠ In this verse, **Matt 6:6**, could Jesus be describing his own praying? Going down into his inner room, resting fully in the present moment, meeting his Father there, and opening himself without reserve to his Father's desire of him, completely at home and fulfilled, and tasting again his Father's meaning at the baptism when his Father said, "You are my Son, whom I love; in you I delight." **(Luke 3:22)**

A sharing in his Sonship and in his praying

✠ Jesus wants us to have a share in this praying of his. He has begun by giving us, through Baptism, a share in his own Sonship. As adopted daughters or sons, we now stand in Jesus' space before the Father, and we are linked to them both by their Spirit. **Our praying begins here.** It is a share in Jesus' own praying.

As we grow into him, that is, into our place with him before the Father, the **way** we pray grows, too, becoming deeper. As we become more involved with him in friendship, allowing him into more layers of our life, he becomes more involved with us and brings our praying into deeper layers of ourself and closer to his praying.

In the earlier stages of prayer, and for a long time, he allows us to contribute our portion: we are **active** in prayer. But he draws us deeper into himself, deeper into our share in his Sonship, and closer to the Father. The result is that **our** contribution becomes less and less, and **his** action is more and more; until eventually, all of the praying in us is done by Jesus and by his Spirit, and we become the **place** for his prayer; we become a temple, a well. This is the desire of Jesus for us; it is the flowering of our baptism. We may safely ask him to do this work in us.

Can I see my Father?

✠Jesus tells me that "my Father" is waiting for me when I enter prayer, waiting for me "in secret", that is, out of sight, beyond my senses. Can I **see** my Father? Yes, and no.

In the earlier stages of prayer, and for a long time, Jesus himself is the image of the Father that I see. Jesus is the full expression, in human terms, of the Father. Then, as Jesus takes over my prayer, images, even of Jesus, stop being of help during prayer. My prayer becomes imageless because it is going deeper, and Jesus is leading me to where there is no image. He leads me to the Father. And what is waiting for me? I meet this Mysterious One, who is the Godhead, the Source of all there is, whom Jesus reveals as loving, tender, caring and welcoming, and as utterly desirable, and as encompassing all the qualities of a mother and a father.

The response

This is my Father; this is the Father of Jesus. **My response**, like that of Jesus, must be one of adoration, awe, before sheer mystery. And like Jesus, too, I **receive** from my Father a share in the utter love that Jesus is receiving from his Father.

Concluding Prayer:

Grant, O Lord, that your love may so fill our lives
that we may count
nothing too small to do for you,
nothing too much to give, and
nothing too hard to bear
for Jesus' sake. Amen.

O Gracious and Holy Father,
give us
Wisdom to perceive you,
Diligence to seek you,
Patience to wait for you,
Eyes to behold you,
A heart to meditate on you,
And a life to proclaim you .
Through the power of the Spirit of Jesus Christ our Lord.
                                        Amen.
                              (Saint Benedict)

Chapter 9

Imagination in Prayer

✠In the previous chapter, I reflected on the teaching of Jesus in Matt. 6:6. From this I spoke about the room, the door, my Father, and the reward. Jesus seemed to be telling of his own experience of prayer. I spoke, also, about our sharing in the Sonship and the praying of Jesus, and of our being brought by him to the mysterious, imageless Father.

Using my imagination so as to become more involved

✠In this chapter, I want to say something about using our imagination during prayer so as to bring it on our side. The steps we have been considering so far in our approach to prayer are all ways of *disposing* ourselves for prayer so as to get ourselves into the right disposition for the meeting with Someone so special. They are ways of gathering ourselves together: one could use the word "**composition**" – **composing** oneself.

The next suggestion of St Ignatius which we will consider is that I compose a mental picture so as to get my imagination involved also in my prayer; this is a further step in "composing myself". Composing a mental picture **composes** me.

In the *Spiritual Exercises*, St Ignatius usually asks us to engage with our imagination **after** the Preparatory Prayer and **before** we ask for what we desire. So **after** asking for the grace of a right overall focus in the Preparatory Prayer, I fix my imagination **before** I fix my desire. In this way, I get my imagination going and on my side at the service of my prayer.

From head to heart

The longest journey for many people is from HEAD to HEART. Prayer that stays in your head doesn't get you personally involved, unless you happen to be the kind of person whose dominant function is thinking, and whose consolations, therefore, come when you experience an insight or a new understanding; and then your heart is touched through the insight and you become quite involved. For this kind of person, understanding leads to strong feelings. They can pray, for instance, with the discourses in St John's Gospel. But for most of us, prayer that stays in the head doesn't get us involved: our feelings remain untouched.

Images evoke feelings

For most of us, the path to our feelings is through our imagination. St Ignatius encourages us to use our imagination so that our feelings will be engaged.

Images evoke feelings. All the advertisers know this. Great amounts of money are spent on image-making, so that our feelings will be drawn. The images of a holiday resort, in a brochure or on a TV advertisement, make you feel you are there in the swimming pool, under the blue sky, among happy, relaxed people, and you begin to want **to be there**. The images of the war in Sarajevo or Iraq or Afghanistan or of the poverty in Rwanda or Haiti cause you to feel **revulsion** and horror, and you want to **turn away**. The images arouse feelings. And we can use images to re-live an experience: when I recall Jacob's Well which I visited during a pilgrimage many years ago, I am back there again winching up the water from 30 metres below and drinking it. It is when our FEELINGS are touched that we are personally involved, and then our prayer becomes an **intimate** experience. Conversely, when there is intimacy happening in our prayer, our feelings are in play at some level, perhaps quite deeply.

Conjecturing the feelings of others

Some people say that they have no power of imagining or have only a poor capacity for creating an image for their prayer. For such people, this suggestion may help. One way of getting our imagination and feelings going is to **conjecture** what feelings the actors in a gospel story or in one from the Old Testament are having.

Say I am praying over the story about Jacob in **Genesis 28:10-22**. I will note Jacob's fear in a strange place as night falls, how he looks around to check whether he is safe: he hears barking and howling from wild animals and becomes tense with fear; he is tired from long miles of walking and eventually falls into a heavy sleep. I note his utter amazement when he awakens from his dream and looks around: his gestures and the look on his face register his feelings; he stands up in wonder and feels stunned. By conjecturing his feelings, I imagine his gestures and am drawn into the scene and I feel with him.

Say I am praying over the scene recounted in **Luke 7: 36-50**. I will observe the cautious and conservative air of the Pharisee, **Simon**, and conjecture his feelings when this woman comes in uninvited: how he draws back in himself; he stiffens up; he is angry at the intrusion by this woman, especially this one. The serving girls are all agog at seeing her, and they are gesturing to each other, stunned, for they know her reputation. I see Simon's embarrassment at how demonstrative the woman is with her tears as she displays such obvious love in public, and here in his dining room, of all places. She is sobbing, and now she is kissing the feet of Jesus; where is this going to stop? Simon feels shocked and affronted and personally threatened, and his disapproval shows in his cross demeanour.

Jesus is surprised, too, but he senses that this love-making has no hook to it: it is transparent. He can feel her feelings through his feet and through his eyes and ears. He has not drawn back; he is calm, but warmly moved. He looks at the woman and seems quite accepting of her kisses and her anointing. He is amazingly free in himself. He has noticed Simon's discomfort but he stays present to what the woman's gestures are saying.

The **woman** is feeling deep gratitude, so much so that she can't wait to express it; she dares to intrude, has eyes only for Jesus. She has met Jesus before somewhere, and meeting him has changed her profoundly. Her tears take her by surprise; she is suddenly overwhelmed by her feelings on being so close to the man who has changed her life and on finding herself accepted again.

By **conjecturing** the feelings of discomfort and surprise and calm acceptance and overwhelming gratitude, I can imagine the **gestures** these evoke and build up enough of a picture. I begin to feel I am there: I become involved.

Projection: I meet myself

✠Images evoke feelings: conjecturing feelings can evoke images. In prayer, I can enter a scene and become an observer or a participant in the story. But there is something else worth noting: some part of myself is **projected** on to the scene. So, when I enter prayer imaginatively like this, I see not only Simon and Jesus and the woman: **I see also myself.**

When I tried to imagine **Simon's** feelings, I was projecting my own feelings on to Simon, for I know what it is like to draw back into myself, to become tense, to feel angry and embarrassed and affronted, and to be disapproving. I was seeing **myself** in Simon.

When I imagined what it was like for **Jesus**, I saw that side also of myself, the side that can accept intimacy, and can notice discomfort in others and can know when expression of affection is sincere.

When I imagined what the **woman** was feeling, I saw the side of myself that knows strong gratitude and the drive to express it, the side that can experience acceptance and self-acceptance, and knows love.

I see Simon and Jesus and the woman through the lenses of experiences I have had. So, when I pray imaginatively, I meet Jesus and the other actors in the scene; and I also meet myself. I meet **both sides** of myself. For instance, (a) the side that can delight in what is going on, that is at home with intimacy, love, union, forgiveness; and (b), the side of myself that is disturbed, ill-at-ease, or challenged, and is in need of healing: the side of me that draws back and judges, or that can't accept forgiveness, or can't accept acceptance, or can't accept the body or affection or touch.

The **gift** for me when I project my feelings in this way,

and meet myself, is that **more of me** is available for the meeting with Jesus in prayer. I am letting him into my genuine self as I am at present, and I am being more intimate, more vulnerable. This allows Jesus to offer me the healing or closeness I have become ready for. It is only what I am **conscious** of that he can heal or change. I may not like what I see of myself, but this is my genuine self at this moment, and it is where Jesus wants to meet me. He meets me only in those places I am **conscious** of. It is important, therefore, not to be afraid to project myself on to a gospel scene or an Old Testament scene, and to meet myself, and to let Jesus meet me there.

Imagination and Prayer Of Faith

✠ There are people, whose prayer has been brought, by God's gift, to a **deeper** place, a level where there are no words or images carrying the interaction with God. It is a dark prayer, which now is more **an attitude**, such as surrender, simple desire, simple longing, waiting, unfocused love ; the feeling here is deep-seated.

This is a *prayer of faith*, a received prayer, and God is the active one. Imagination can have no direct role in their praying. Trying to be active by using their imagination during prayer would *block* prayer. So, what are they to do?

They can use their imagination, not during full prayer but only **outside** of prayer, when they are actively reflecting on, say, a gospel scene.

Concluding Prayer:

> *Lord, be the beginning and end of all we do and say.*
> *Prompt our actions with your grace,*
> *and complete them with your all-powerful help.*
> *We ask this through Christ our Lord. Amen.*

Jesus,
may all that is you flow into me.
May your body and blood be my food and drink.
May your passion and death be my strength and life.
Jesus,
with you by my side enough has been given.
May the shelter I seek be the shadow of your cross.
Let me not run from the love which you offer,
but hold me safe from the forces of evil.
On each of my dyings shed your light and your love.
Keep calling to me until that day comes
when, with your saints, I may praise you forever. Amen.
(paraphrase of Anima Christi *by David Fleming S.J.)*

Chapter 10

Desire in Prayer

✤In the previous chapter, I spoke about the use of our imagination in prayer. I compose a mental picture in order to compose myself and to get my imagination involved and on my side during prayer. Images, I said, evoke feelings, and when my feelings are engaged I am more involved. I suggested that a way of getting our imagination to work for us is by conjecturing the feelings of the actors in a gospel scene. In prayer with our imagination we meet not only the Lord and the others in the story: we meet ourselves, too, for we project our own feelings and past experiences onto them. We become more available to Jesus; he can heal what I become conscious of in myself. I noted that the active use of the imagination does not have a place in Prayer of Faith.

Desire in prayer

✤In this chapter, I want to move on to the fifth step in prayer suggested by St Ignatius, which is, that I ask for what I want. Desire in prayer is a large topic, so I can say only a little about it in these few pages.

It may seem strange that telling God what I want is included among the recommended approaches to prayer; but we learn from the gospels that Jesus himself invited people to name and ask their desire:

✤ To John and Andrew: "What are you looking for?" (John 1:38)

✤ To Bartimaeus: "What do you want me to do for you? " (Mark 10:51)

✤ To the Woman at the Well: "If you only knew what God is offering and who it is that is saying to you, 'Give me something to drink', you would have been the one to ask, and he would have given you living water." (John 4:10)

In my approaches to prayer, I have already got in touch with how I am feeling; here now I am getting in touch with my desiring. Jesus, when giving his teaching on prayer in Luke 11:1-13, said that we are to ASK, SEEK, KNOCK, and he assured us that our Father in heaven is more than willing to give us good gifts, even the Holy Spirit, "to those who ask him." Note that Jesus names the Holy Spirit as the gift that the Father particularly wants us to have, who are his children by adoption through our baptism, but he teaches that we are to **ask** for this gift, and this gift above all others.

Who is the Holy Spirit? In the Trinity, there is a bond of love between the Father and the Son which is so total, so complete, that this love is a third person; we call this Person the Holy Spirit. In relation to the Father and the Son, the Spirit is the love bonding them together in utter oneness. In relation to **us**, the Spirit, who is this bond of love, connects us, too, in love, with the Father and with Jesus: we are made sons and daughters of God and are brought within the domain of the Trinity. In this space, the Spirit is our **Enabler** to help us be who we are, sons and daughters of God. The Spirit enables us: to see what only faith can see; to grow in faith; to pray as children of God; to love and accept love; to grow in personal knowledge of God and in desire for God; to become more fully the friends of Jesus.

What Jesus **treasures** most for himself is his own union, as Son, with his Father, the union brought about by the Holy Spirit. He wants us, too, to have a **share** in this treasure, but he invites us to ask, so that we can have more and more of the Spirit. In asking, we become ready to receive. Our asking can, of course, be continual, done again and again, for this bond can grow deeper and deeper. Do I want a growing union with my Lord?

THE FIFTH STEP ~ naming the desire and asking for it
✠ In view of all this, it seems appropriate, therefore, that St Ignatius, in the *Spiritual Exercises*, should say, "I ask God for what I desire." In the *Exercises*, this asking is for what belongs to my relationship with the Lord: you could say that this asking is about "us", the Lord and me. I ask for what I want for **our relationship**.

Now, it is one thing to desire: it is quite another thing to **ask** for what I desire, for the asking makes a significant difference. The asking focuses my desire, and it also opens me to receive what I ask for. Consequently, this fifth step in the approach to prayer is a matter of focusing my desire. What do I want? I name it to myself **and** I ask the Lord for it.

The fundamental desire
We arrive at prayer carrying desire. In our essential core,

we are one huge desire for God. It manifests itself in our quest for happiness, and in our discovering that no particular object has the power ultimately to satisfy us. Sooner or later, our restlessness returns and we go searching again for the ultimate satisfaction – another name for God – but it won't be found on this side of the grave. "You have made us for yourself", wrote St Augustine in his *Confessions*, "and our hearts are restless until they rest in you." (Book I, I)

This fundamental desire is always at work in us. It is bigger in scope than any particular object of desire: its scope is unlimited; its fulfilment is God. But we are not pure spirit: we are body as well as spirit. Therefore, in actual practice, we have to desire things that are limited: we desire 'this' or 'that'; we focus our desiring on something finite or limited. This focusing brings into play the **unfocused** fundamental desire which is towards God. In this way, the infinite level of desire and finite level work together. Our fundamental infinite desiring always accompanies a desire for some particular object. When I want' this' or 'that' object of desire, I am also wanting God, though unconsciously. Our desiring is always comprised of two levels, the unlimited level at my core and the particular level, like two sides of one coin. This is the way we are made.

The deep down longing for God is intrinsic to our being. We can't get away from it. But we can proceed to **mask** that yearning with busyness, pleasures, superficiality, the drive for power, the greed for possessions, "the cares and riches and pleasures of life" that Jesus speaks of in the parable of the seed landing on the four kinds of ground in Luke 8:4-15. We can **hide** from our deep longing for God; we can **misinterpret** its meaning, turn elsewhere for satisfaction; we can stay **superficial**; but it will not go away; it is waiting to be heard. This fundamental yearning for God is part of our very being. Once this deep place has been touched and awakened – perhaps around the end of adolescence – we are looking unconsciously for a conscious relationship with the Infinite Mystery who is God.

Will the Preparatory Prayer be enough?

✢ In the 3rd step of our approaches to prayer, the Preparatory Prayer, I asked for the grace to be directed to the praise and service of God in all I do. There I was asking for the grace that my fundamental desire towards God be **effectively** present in all I do, and particularly now in my prayer. Will this not be enough to steer me forward? Will it be enough that I am desiring as full an openness towards God as I can muster, and then proceed? Why is St Ignatius telling me to specify my desire?

Desire needs to be specified

Our desiring is complex. Full open desire may well fit a person who has been stretched, by a long graced process, to let the Spirit do the praying. Such a one is now **consciously** carrying the Spirit's inarticulate desire for the Father that Paul speaks of in Romans 8: 15, 26, a gift which began **unconsciously** in baptism. Such a person is asked simply to be the place of this prayer. It is entirely a received prayer. But until prayer takes on this openly mystical flow and form, there is a great need for me to specify my desire in prayer, as St Ignatius suggests, because my desiring is not only infinite in scope, but, when specified, is complex. So I need to pay attention to my desiring and see what is going on there.

Mixed Motives

This need becomes evident when we remember that prayer is a relationship, and that desire is at the heart of it. We are well aware that in a human relationship we can have hidden intentions or motives which disturb the flow of communication and love between us, and can cause hurt, until we bring them to the surface.

It is the same with prayer. We arrive at our prayer time carrying a jumble of motives which need to be brought to the surface, and sorted out, or at least admitted to. "What do I really want from this interaction with God?" "Are my intentions in tune with God's?" "Or are I and God at cross-purposes here?"

During prayer, how much of **my own agenda** is going on? My need to feel good? My need for achievement? My fear of closeness? My fear of feelings? Am I clinging to my method of prayer out of fear of failure in prayer or from my need for control?

Can I be here **on God's terms**? Can I raise my concern off myself and desire instead to know who God is and what he wants of me and for me?

Outside of prayer, is there a significant disharmony between me and God in some area of my life e.g. relationships, justice or honesty? What is my conscience telling me? Do I really want God in my life? Am I open to what God might want to ask of me and to give to me?

Why am I praying? To honour God? To know God and his will? Or mainly for myself? Or only when I am in trouble? Always asking and never thanking? Am I using God? Say, as a security blanket?

We need to remember that Jesus is our teacher and model of prayer. Prayer "in Jesus' name" is prayer that is in accord with his attitudes and values. To pray "in Jesus' name" I must get into line with what God also wants from it, for God too, has desires. This prayer time is a meeting, not only of God and me, but is also a meeting-place of our desires, God's and mine.

A meeting-place of desires

God desires me: that is why I exist. So when I enter prayer, I come under this immense radiation of desire. God is here drawing me to himself, longing to reveal himself to me. This is God's great desire, and it is why he sent his only Son to be his Word to us.

For my part, I desire God, especially if I am moving beyond wanting God's gifts to wanting God for himself. This desire in me is God's work: "No one can come to me," said Jesus, "unless drawn by the Father who sent me." (John 6:44) In this relationship between God and me, there is mutual desire. Prayer gives expression to this mutual desire.

Our experience of desires

✠ As we have emphasised, our desiring is complex. Let us look more closely at our experience of desire. Someone has wisely said that desires are what surface when our needs are met. I need sleep; I need to get out of the cold; I need shelter; I need a drink; I need food; but to eat and drink with someone is my desire.

When we look closely at our experience of desire, we note that each of us is a bundle of desires. We have desires for love, companionship, acceptance; desires for meaning, for success; we desire to be significant, to have power, to be in control; we have sexual desires, desires for union, for parenthood; and beneath all this, we have desire for God. You could say that all our desires are **veiled** desires for God; our hearts are restless until they rest in God, for he has made us for himself.

Some of our desires are relational, and others are not. Some are deep, others superficial. Some can destroy ourselves, while others bring out the best in us. There is enormous energy in our desiring, and it requires to be harnessed by a wise discipline. Prayer can afford this discipline and right direction.

A divided heart

Some of our desires are in conflict. We find ourselves wanting options that are irreconcilable. We cannot have everything, for one choice can exclude some other possible option. Often I don't know what I want, and, more than often, the real motives lurking in my actual desires are hidden from me. It is a puzzling and confusing scene.

Consequently, there is need for discernment of my desire in order to see what mixture is present and to find healing for it. This desiring heart of mine is warped and wounded. I am slow to see what is truly good; my ego-centred self conflicts with my authentic self and blinds me. The better choice often requires that I accept some pain as I choose to resist my self-centred demands, but this is not easy.

Who will heal me of this division so that my desires don't wreak havoc and ruin myself and others? The Lord tells us through Jeremiah, "The heart is devious above all else; it is perverse – who can understand it?" (Jeremiah 17:9) Where will I find healing? In the end, this healing is God's work, and personal prayer is a good place in which to receive the Lord's healing presence. "I, the Lord, search the heart, test the motives" (Jer. 17:10) The Lord heals me by drawing my heart more and more towards himself: he heals me through my desires.

The question is: by which desires? The answer is: by my **authentic** desires. These are the ones closest to the fundamental desire in each of us for God. They are likely to bring me to my true destination. How do I find them?

Levels of desire

In each of us, there are deep desires and superficial ones. We need to get the levels into order so that the deeper ones are heard by us and given primary place. I believe that the way to put order into our desires is to tap into the deeper ones; these will **relativise** the superficial ones and put them into their proper place, and also modify their power over us.

Authentic desires

Our deeper desires are likely to be our authentic ones, desires that are true to who we are. When you name and also enter your authentic desire, it will settle you because it is coming from a deep place inside you. And because it comes from deep inside you, it is likely to be a desire in harmony with God, even a desire implanted in you by God. Our authentic desires have certain characteristics. They are relational. They draw us beyond mere self-interest. They lead us into self-donation. They draw us beyond the boundaries of ego-self. In a word, they express what is best in us.

God leads us by our desires. He leads us to himself. He has made us for himself. Our deepest desire is for union with God. Our authentic desires connect us with that fundamental drive, and bring us to the "living water" of conscious relationship with Jesus, about which he spoke to the Samaritan woman at the well. (John 4:10) Conscious relationship with Jesus heals our wounded divided heart.

Finding authentic desire through prayer

To find my authentic desires through prayer, I must experiment with my desires to discover which ones settle me and bring me into the peace of connectedness with God. I go beyond thinking about them: I **enter** them, try them out in prayer, and then observe their effect **in** me. God has implanted in us a longing for him. My authentic desires will harmonise with that fundamental longing and bring peace.

A journey of desire

Desire seems to match personal growth, Though God desires to reveal himself to me and draw me close, I may not be ready for this yet. Though God desires to give himself to me, I may not be able to welcome him yet. Though God desires to communicate personally with me, I may not be ready to hear him. There is development in my desiring. I am where I am, but God will draw me forward.

Take as an example the gospel story of Bartimaeus' faith in Jesus as recounted in Mark 10:46-52. Initially, Bartimaeus' desire was to get his sight back. His need opened him to look to Jesus with faith. He brought his desire to Jesus, asked and received. The first person he saw with his new-found sight was Jesus. Something happened in that eye-to-eye meeting. A new desire was awakened: he began to follow Jesus "on the way". This "way" was leading Jesus to Jerusalem and to his passion, death and resurrection. These words, "the way", became the first description of Christian discipleship. Bartimaeus' initial desire had developed into a much deeper desire, bringing him to make Jesus the centre of his life. (It must be significant that this man's name has become part of the gospel tradition.) Bartimaeus was on a journey of desire.

Desire and Jesus

Finally, a word about Jesus. Jesus was a man of great desires. He was in touch with the deepest level of human desire in himself. His deepest desires centred on his relationship with his Father: they gave direction to his life.

For our part, our deepest desires are activated by our relationship with Jesus, for he is the **answer** to our core longing. When that deep level is alive in us and directed towards him, it relativises the less deep levels of desire in us that bother us; it gives us a control and a freedom around important human issues, such as, insecurity, disapproval, disempowerment, and sexuality. Relationship with him is our deep security; the approval we most need is from him; our surrender to him in love empowers us; and our sexual drive becomes a Godward energy embedded in our fundamental desire for God. We get our levels of desire into order when we tap into our deepest levels: and these are about Jesus.

In conclusion: St John of the Cross underlined the key importance of desire in our relationship with God when he wrote: "It is worthy of note that God does not place his grace in the soul except according to its desire and love." (*Spiritual Canticle* 13, 12)

Concluding Prayer:

> *Lord God of power and might,*
> *nothing is good which is against your will,*
> *and all is of value which comes from your hand.*
> *Place in our hearts a desire to please you*
> *and fill our minds with insight into love,*
> *so that every thought may grow in wisdom*
> *and all our efforts be filled with your peace.*
> *We ask this through Christ our Lord. Amen.*
>
> *(Missal, 22nd Sunday)*

Father,
I abandon myself into your hands ;
Do with me what you will.
Whatever you may do, I thank you :
I am ready for all, I accept all.
Let only your will be done
in me and in all your creatures.
I wish no more than this, O Lord.
Into your hands I commend my soul ;
I offer it to you with all the love of my heart,
for I love you, Lord, and so need
to give myself,
to surrender myself,
into your hands,
without reserve
and with boundless confidence,
for you are my Father, Amen.
(Prayer of Abandonment *of Charles de Foucauld*)

Chapter 11

Disappointment in Prayer: invitation to depth

✤In the previous chapter I explored the topic of DESIRE in prayer. I spoke about naming my desire and asking for it in prayer. Our desiring is complex for our heart is wounded. Our authentic desires are our truly human ones, and they are likely to be from God, and in harmony with God's own desires for us. To discover them I suggested that we experiment with our desires, bringing them before God in prayer and discerning their harmonious effect on us. I spoke about desire and Jesus: Jesus is the answer to our deepest desires.

Disappointment in Prayer

In this chapter, I move away from the topic of desire to discuss a feeling that we all have had sometime, the feeling that prayer has gone "badly". I am referring to disappointment in prayer. Perhaps my experience is of putting a lot of time and effort into prayer, but still I find that it doesn't seem to work: I continue to be inundated with involuntary distractions. I prepare the subject matter for prayer beforehand, and I also prepare my own self by the way I enter prayer, as St Ignatius suggests, but despite all this care, I have the feeling that something is wrong. I am disappointed.

What do I do with this?

What do you do with disappointment in prayer? Do you hide the feeling from yourself and stay fixated in your way of praying? Or do you give up personal prayer? Or, on the other hand, do you pay attention to your feeling of disappointment and let it lead you to question that old style of praying that is not working for you, and query some of your assumptions about prayer, and start considering new approaches? Do you, for instance, see prayer as something static, a fixed pattern, or do you see prayer as a **changing experience**, as a journey with Someone who relates differently to you according as you grow in spiritual maturity?

Finding freedom

I have two images.

1) One is of a **bumble-bee** in a room, flying repeatedly

against the upper pane of glass in one of those old-fashioned sash windows that you can move up and down. It sees where it wants to go — out there — but finds itself blocked mysteriously. Eventually the bumble-bee drops down exhausted on the ledge across that upper pane, and then slips out through the space between the two parts of the window, and now finds itself in a free and open space.

2) The other image is of a **hare** being pursued by greyhounds. There is one opening in the fence at the far end of a long field. Until it finds that opening, it is utterly frustrated by the fence; it can't make progress; it feels blocked and imprisoned. But when it does find that one opening, it goes through into freedom and open space, and feels safe.

The **bumble-bee** attains freedom when it gives up all the fruitless effort, and just rests.

The **hare** finds freedom when it moves along the fence and finds the opening at last: it has tried various places in search of that opening.

From effort to receptivity

What could be the **difficulty** in the prayer of a person who is experiencing disappointment? Could it be that I am still looking upon prayer as **a task**, as a skill to be mastered? Most of us who are idealistic are motivated by a need to achieve and the need to be in control; but when we bring this attitude to bear upon prayer, we are sure to encounter difficulty and disappointment, for prayer is a **relationship**. And the stronger our orientation towards achievement, the greater will be our disappointment and our sense of failure. Failure is hard to take; failure is hard to talk about and admit to, so we may never seek help.

Perhaps, as in the case of the bumble-bee, there is a change called for, a change **from** effort **to** receptivity, to a receptivity that takes the shape of giving-in, of letting go of control, of looking to God, of listening to God. But the very **first step** could be to acknowledge the unwelcome feelings around the disappointment.

How well do I listen?

Prayer, instead of being a task, is part of a relationship in which I allow the Other to have my time, to claim my attention on his terms, and to require that I listen to him, and, especially, that I wait for him.

It might be helpful for me to reflect on how I am outside of prayer, and to ask myself what I am like in my way of relating with other persons. This may give me an insight into how I am relating with God, both in prayer and in life. For instance, do I let people claim my time and my attention? Do I let myself look at them and listen to them? Or am I so much caught up in my own moods and issues that I am unable to pay real attention to my friends? Do I want only to have my own say? Is it hard for me to hear somebody out until she or he is finished? Am I ever willing to let myself be displaced and to make room for another person by listening well?

Displacement

If prayer is going to become deep, I will indeed experience **displacement of my ego-self**. God will do this. God will empty me, both outside of prayer and inside prayer, so that he can fill me with more of his presence. But God will need my cooperation if God is to achieve this.

God coming closer

I suggest that the experience of disappointment in prayer could be a signal that God is moving closer and telling you that he wants to make room for himself in you.

I remember a TV advertisement for a credit card that the Bank of Ireland ran in the 1980's. They called this credit card an ACCESS card. The advert ran "Your ACCESS card puts you in control". Applying this to prayer, I say the opposite; I say that if prayer is deepening, then "Your ACCESS to God puts you OUT of control". When prayer is going deep, the call is to let prayer be less controlled, and even to seem like helpless disarray ; a call to let prayer be done in me by Another ; a call to value be-ing more than do-ing ; a call to accept that fewer words, or even silence, are enough for holding me in his presence. It may even be a call to acknowledge more deeply than before that I don't ever need to earn God's love, and that my effort to make what I think is perfect prayer is blocking God from showing me that he is loving me beyond my deserts with an unearned love. It may be that I am afraid to let myself experience my helplessness and utter poverty before God when I pray. Is it alright for me to feel poor in prayer and to be there unprotected before God ? Maybe I have to stop monitoring and assessing my performance in prayer, and hand it over to God. Let me let go of the satisfaction that I used to have of seeing myself successful in prayer in my own estimation.

Brought deeper

Better now to take my eyes off myself and to let God be in charge and for me to be in prayer **on God's terms.** Better now to let TIME be my sacrificial lamb which I waste and put beyond usefulness to myself. Better now to trust my helplessness and my poverty. I am being brought down below the level of my ideas and images and words to a level of **faith** where I am connected with God mysteriously. And then, when I let myself become less busy and more sensitive inside myself, I will pick up hints that God is indeed here, connecting with me: this is faith, the connection between God and me in a place deep inside me.

I am being brought down, like that bumble-bee, below the window pane of my clear ideas and great effort, and led out into a new atmosphere where my prayer will be **God's work**, not mine.

Concluding Prayer

Thank you, Lord Jesus, for this time of prayer.
I accept whatever way it went for me.
Help me to recognise your gift in it.
Train me by your Spirit to grow in prayer.
You are always greater, drawing me ever forward.
Take me with you into the presence of your Father.
                                                    Amen.

We shall become Christians when we weep,
not because we have lost something,
but because we were given so much.

(From a parish bulletin in Toronto, 1987)

Take, Lord, and receive
all my liberty, my memory, my understanding
and my entire will,
all that I have and possess.

You gave it all to me; to you I give it back.
All is yours, dispose of it entirely according to your will.
Give me only the grace to love you,
for that is enough for me.
(St Ignatius Loyola)

Chapter 12

Reflecting and Relating in Prayer

In the previous chapter, I reflected on the experience of disappointment in prayer and suggested that it might be a signal inviting us to go deeper, and to become receptive, and to hand over more of the control to God. For prayer is a relationship in which the Lord wants to take over, so as to give more of himself to me. He wants to bring me closer and deeper, below the level where words, images and ideas have been serving my prayer, down to another level, the level of faith, where God can engage with me without intermediary. I gave the example of a bumble-bee at a window dropping down exhausted from its fruitless effort and unexpectedly finding itself out in a free and open space through no effort of its own. I said that when prayer is developing my access to God puts me out of control. Disappointment in prayer could be telling me that God is inviting me to become contemplative in the sense of praying in faith and, therefore, to be in fact closer to God.

From reflecting to relating

✠ Here I want to focus again on the time of prayer and share something more from the wisdom of St Ignatius.

Since prayer is a personal meeting between God and me, then I need to distinguish between my reflecting on a text of Scripture and the actual meeting, the actual I-Thou encounter which my reflecting is meant to bring me to. To ensure that this transition happens, St Ignatius, in the *Spiritual Exercises*, speaks of a "colloquy", a word which comes from the Latin and means a "talk-with" or a response on my part. He says "A colloquy is made, properly speaking, in the way a friend speaks to another or a servant to one in authority." (#54) He suggests that we conclude our prayer time with a talk-with, a response, a direct meeting; but in practice this can happen naturally at other points in the prayer period too. The danger for me is that I could find myself immersed in my reflections on a text or scene, enjoying my exploration of meaning, and yet not meeting the Lord himself; I could even be avoiding such a meeting.

A meeting is essential to prayer. So this suggestion from Ignatius is about making sure that the meeting happens, that at some point during prayer one moves **from** reflecting **to** relating, from thinking to person-to-person encounter, from ideas to involvement, from head to heart, from observing to engaging with, from being an observer on the outside to being a participant on the inside. It is to ensure that a descent is made to the level of personal engagement with the Lord. It is a moment of intimacy. It can be short or long. It can be wordless. It can be restful. And it doesn't have to be confined to the end of the prayer time.

If I use words, I speak from where I am at in myself. Say, for example, I am affected by the word "precious" in Isaiah 43:4, "You are precious in my eyes and I love you". I tell the Lord how I am affected. I may say, "I am not able to accept that I could be precious to you"; or on the other hand, I may find myself glad at knowing and feeling that I am "precious" to the Lord, and I may want to respond with "Thank You", or "Yes, I accept that I am precious to you, and I want to believe it more deeply". Having spoken, I might then wait for a response of some kind from the Lord, for a response may well be given, in some form.

Closure
✠ A final suggestion from St Ignatius (#54 and throughout the *Spiritual Exercises*) is that I conclude my time of prayer with the Our Father. It is the Lord's own prayer, his gift to us, so to say it is a gesture of gratitude, and it brings me to the Father. It helps me to put a closure on my time of prayer. Sometimes, I may come away from prayer thinking, "Well, at least I have said an Our Father"!

Concluding Prayer

Thanks be to you, my Lord Jesus Christ,
for all the benefits which you have given me,
for all the pains and insults you have borne for me.

O most merciful redeemer, Friend and Brother,
may I know you more clearly,
love you more dearly,
and follow you more nearly.

(The Prayer of St Richard, Bishop of Chichester, 1245-1253)

Chapter 13

Learning from Prayer

When prayer is over: review

✦When prayer is over, it is **wise** to look back over how it went. It is also a **gracious** thing to do, for it is a way of showing appreciation to the One who has visited me in my heart; I need to remind myself that this was no ordinary meeting, even if it takes place every day.

This review is made **after** the prayer so that I won't be monitoring my prayer while praying. Postponing my reflection on the prayer allows me to enter more fully into the experience of prayer.

Prupose of the review

The review has two purposes: (i) I want to **learn** from my experience; (ii) I want to know what to pray on in the **next period**, guided by what happened; here I am speaking of what is called repetition or revisiting in prayer.

Prayer is a **skill**. I learn how to do it by doing it — like learning to see or ride a bicycle or swim. I learn how to do it **better** by reflecting on it afterwards.

Prayer is always an **adapting** of myself to Someone greater, Someone mysterious, whom I can never control or bring down to my size. In prayer, I am God's dance-partner, as it were, where God is always the one taking the initiative ; so I am always learning how to adjust right now to God's movement in me, for God is greater and is always stretching me. Prayer is never mastered. It is a gift given in the moment, unpredictable.

Prayer is always **changing**; it is full of surprises, it is a journey, a journey across a vast ocean ; prayer is never at a standstill.

Prayer is **unique**. Each one of us can say about our prayer, "My prayer is unique to me, for my relationship with God is unique, and God's relationship with me is unique, too". However, it would probably be more accurate to speak of prayer as "our prayer" – God's and mine – than of "my prayer".

What St Ignatius says

Here is what St Ignatius says in the *Spiritual Exercises* (#77) about review of prayer:

"After an exercise is finished (i.e. the prayer time)... I will either sit down or walk around for a quarter of an hour and consider **how things went with me** in the meditation or contemplation. **If things went poorly with me**, I will look for the cause, and having found it, I will be sorry, so that I may do better in the future. **If things went well with me**, I will give thanks to God our Lord, and the next time try to follow the same method."

It is recommended that the review be done in a different place from the prayer – note the "walking" – and it would be good to take notes.

Note that the question, "how things went with me" is expressed **receptively**. The question for me is more about what happened to me, what happened *in* me, during the hour, the way I was moved or was agitated, whether I experienced something as energising or disenergising, whether I received some spiritual insight or was given greater clarity. In other words, I try to note what response was drawn from me when God worked upon me.

The review

a) What does it mean to say that "**things went well with me**" in the prayer? **Some examples:**

  i) I experienced **connectedness**: I was engaged by something that held my attention, or I felt repelled or challenged by something I didn't want to face.

ii) Prayer **flowed**: I sensed it fitted me; there was a flow of energy, of awareness; I experienced freedom.

iii) I felt **affected** in some way; I sensed it was God acting on me.

iv) I received the **grace** I asked for: felt knowledge, love, sorrow, openness, trust, surrender, union, etc.

v) I **found** courage, hope, spiritual insight, greater clarity, peace.

vi) I was drawn away **from** self-preoccupation, self-concern, (but not necessarily from self-awareness)

vii) I had a sense of **meeting** the Lord, a sense of presence

viii) I felt **settled**; I had a sense of at-home-ness.

b) What does it mean to say that "**things went poorly for me**" in prayer? **Some examples:**

i) I had peace when I started, but I **lost** it: why?

ii) It was all **bland**; nothing at all engaged ; I felt "turned off".

iii) I stayed in my **head**; I didn't engage with the Lord; I didn't let myself meet the Lord.

iv) I got turned in **on myself**; I became the focus. (This is not the same as feeling challenged or repelled.). I got drawn away from the relationship with the Lord.

v) I was **restless**; I felt like abandoning the prayer. (The reason may be that I was trying to do something that didn't suit me, or that I was being too active. Abbot John Chapman's advice is: "Pray as you can, not as you can't".)

vi) The Lord seemed **distant**, or absent.

vii) I couldn't get **started**.

Possible causes

i) I rushed into prayer; I didn't prepare myself.

ii) I acted as if the prayer depended all on me.

iii) I didn't get in touch with my own self; was absent from myself.

iv) I was too active, leaving no space for God; I stayed in control.

v) My focus was not right: I was in it more for myself than for God.

vi) I drew back from the intimacy that was offered.

vii) The Lord wants to teach me something about how to be in prayer.

A gift

When things go **poorly** with me in prayer, there may be **a gift** in this experience for me from God: God may be teaching me to remember that prayer is his gift, and that I am to be humble and to ask to be taught by him how to pray. We can **learn** much when things go wrong. If I discover where I was to blame when things went poorly with me, I remember to tell the Lord I am sorry.

The next time of prayer

In my **review**, I note **where** I was engaged, I note **where** I felt challenged, I note **where** I felt a sense of at-home-ness. These places in the subject-matter of my prayer are what I should **return** to in my **next period**, especially if the movement was strong.

Chapter 14
The Next Time of Prayer

✠Having learnt from my review of prayer how to go about it well, I am now in a position to take guidance for what to pray on in the next time of prayer. My focus shifts to the **content** of prayer. This is the second purpose of the review.

I want to know **what** to pray on in the next period, guided by what has happened. I am speaking of what is called **repetition** or revisiting in prayer. My review may reveal to me some **point** in the previous material which is still alive for me. This affords a certain continuity in prayer. Repetition also helps us to listen more attentively to the Lord and to go deeper.

A few examples

a) I was praying over the scene in **Luke 5** about the call of Peter and his companions. In my review, I noticed that I was struck by three words in verse 2, "washing their nets", and had seen that Jesus came to them when they were doing something quite ordinary. I noticed, too, that I felt contentment at that point, which is not usual for me. So in my next period of prayer, I return to this **material** to see if the Lord wishes to say more to me.

b) I was praying over **Revelation 3:20**. In my review, I noticed that I felt afraid at the words, "hears my voice and opens the door"; it was a definite discomfort. Then, an insight came in the form of a remembered line from **Isaiah 43**, "I have called you by name; you are mine", and my fear gave way to desire to open myself to Jesus. So in the next period of prayer, I return to the same **material** to see if the Lord wishes to deepen my desire.

These two examples illustrate where I **return** to in my next time of prayer, namely, to the place or material where I experienced a notable affective movement that was welcome during prayer. I return to where I felt **consoled**. Welcome movements, such as a strong sense of God's presence, an unexpected peace, a surge of desire, a sense of joy, a new insight, are examples of spiritual consolation. I return to the places where notable consolation occurred, for they are linking me with God

c) I have been praying over the testing of Jesus in the wilderness after his baptism. In my review, I noticed that I could not get started, but was filled with distractions and anxiety. So in the next period of prayer, I return to the same **material**. Something is alive for me there, but I am experiencing it as a block : I must face into it to let the Lord overcome my barriers.

d) I have been praying over the scene in the house of Simon the Pharisee recounted in **Luke 7**. In my review, I noticed that verse 44 stood out for me: "I came into your house". I felt arrested by this. I felt challenged. Jesus has come into my house. I am resisting his coming. I am like Simon, not giving myself to Jesus. The woman came with open heart, gave herself over. I feel asked by Jesus not to hold back. But can I? In the next time of prayer, I will revisit the same **material**, for it is still alive for me.

e) I was using my imagination in praying over the healing story in **John 5**. In my review, I noticed that I was struck by the fact that it was Jesus who made the approach and offer to the sick man in verse 6; the man himself did not ask. I sense that Jesus was also asking me, "Do you want to get well?" I was aware of fear. I find it hard to trust. Something is holding me back. In my next time of prayer, I will revisit that question of Jesus, for it is still alive for me. It is where the Spirit is at work. It would not be right for me to focus on some other point instead.

Examples c) to e) illustrate a different experience in prayer: I felt an **unwelcome** affective movement that I found challenging. I must return to this material, for it is alive for me. If I don't return to it, prayer will become flat and unconnected. Challenging or unwelcome experiences in prayer tend to be instances of **spiritual desolation**: they tend to draw me back from where God is present. Other examples are: moments of struggle, a feeling of unease, a sense of God's absence, a feeling of self-doubt and helplessness. I **return** to the places where the desolation occurred so that the Lord will overcome the barriers in me causing the feeling of desolation

What not to return to

1) It is important to distinguish between the welcome or unwelcome **feeling** and the **material** that occasioned it. I **don't** return to the **feeling** itself in an attempt to revive it. I return to those **points** in the material I was praying on where the welcome or unwelcome feeling occurred.
2) When it is a case of **spiritual desolation**, I need to distinguish the desolate **feeling** from the desolate thoughts brought on by the feeling. I don't return to the **thoughts** caused by the unwelcome feeling. I return to the **material** that occasioned the feeling.
3) I don't return to material that I experienced as **bland**. The Spirit is not using it just now to carry his presence to me; maybe at another time he will.

Repetition (revisiting) is not

✢ going over the material again to understand it better as in preparing for an exam;

✠ going back to the same text to dig up something new ;
✠ returning to ALL the material of the last period of prayer

But repetition (revisiting) is

✠ returning to those **points** where "I have experienced new insight or greater consolation or desolation or greater spiritual relish". (*Sp Ex* #62 and #118)

Benefits of repetition (revisiting)

✠ It **allows** movements in prayer to take place. Going from one passage to another successively can **cut off** such movement.
✠ It sharpens my ability to **notice** interior movements. Many of my reactions at prayer happen without my noticing them, so repetition gives time for these reactions to be felt more distinctly when they happen again.
✠ Through repetition I learn to **listen** more attentively to God.
✠ Repetition helps desolation turn into consolation. Often when God is trying to communicate with me at a deeper level, I may be **resisting** him, and this shows up as distraction, struggle and boredom. If I return to the points I first experienced as desolation, I often find that the Lord has overcome **my barriers**, and the desolation gives way to consolation, struggle to surrender, darkness to light.
✠ Repetition helps my prayer to become **simpler**, covering less ground, going down in depth. I become more receptive to God's action and truly contemplative and surrendered.

Chapter 15

When the Next Time of Prayer is NOT a Repetition: be led by DESIRE

Say I have stayed with the prayer material I was using until I was **satisfied**, as Ignatius recommends. Repetition, then, is not the next step. But where do I go next? How will I choose? Will I just open another text at random to see if it connects me with the Lord in prayer? Will I look up the Mass texts for today or for Sunday?

Engage with desire

✠ My suggestion is that we should begin, not with a text, but with our **desire**, for the Lord leads us by our own desires. Our fundamental desire, implanted in us by him, is desire for God; it springs up in us from deep down; it is there even when we are not adverting to it. It is probably better, then, to consult with myself first and identify the **particular** desire that is present in me, and then choose a text that relates to this desire.

This is the principle that is at work in the *Spiritual Exercises* of **St Ignatius**. Ignatius gets us to engage with a progressive movement of desire: in this way desire shapes the journey of the *Exercises*. The two essential elements in any period of prayer in the *Exercises* are:

(i) my asking for what I want, and (ii) my personal meeting or conversation with the Lord. The points or text that I pray with are the means or bridge that link up my desire with my meeting.

Journey of desire

✠ In the *Exercises*, the journey of **desire** begins with openness to God's love. Everyone wants to be loved. Prayer with texts about God's providential care for me — my graced history — enlarges my trust and expands my **desire** to accept God's offer of a personal relationship with him. I grow in my response of love; I desire to place him in the centre of my heart. Then, with so much light coming in, revealing God's goodness to me, something else begins to be revealed to me, namely, my own lack of response, my shadow-side, how much of self-interest is at work in my choices and how unworthy I am of friendship with my loving Lord. In the presence of God's love still coming to me, I face my sinfulness and I **desire** forgiveness and ask for the gift of sorrow. Prayer over God's mercy reveals to me a new face of God and I discover that I am a sinner loved and forgiven, because Jesus is my Saviour.

This discovery may next evoke a **desire** to draw closer to Jesus, who has accepted me, and to know and love him more and to be with him as his follower. My prayer brings me through the life story of Jesus in the gospels and draws me into an ever deeper **desire** to make him the centre of my own story.

Prayer moves on into the story of his passion and death for us. I **desire** the gift of compassion, staying present to him in his sufferings because he is my friend and Lord, and also growing, perhaps unknown to myself, in my compassion for others who suffer.

When I come to the stories of his resurrection, I am glad for Jesus' victory over suffering and death, and I **desire** the gift of intense joy because of his great joy. I want to be happy for *him*: this is a gift without self-reference.

This long journey of **desire** is a journey of **relationship**. Any of those phases of desire can be further deepened during my life. Our task is to identify **our current desire** and to let it guide us in our prayer.

Led by my desire

✠ The Lord is mysteriously drawing me to himself, and so I may find that my current **desire** is to **open myself** to his love and to let him into my life more. There are many texts that would be attractive to me when my desire is set in this direction, such as: Isaiah 43:1-7, Hosea 2:14-20 (JB 16-22), Jeremiah 29:10-14, Lamentations 3:17-26, Deuteronomy 7:6-9, Psalms 23, 40, 62, 63, 139, Matthew 11:28-30, Luke 12:22-34, John 15:9-17, to quote just a few.

Consciousness of my sinfulness could direct my **desire** to seeking **forgiveness**, and my prayer would be helped by texts such as, Mark 1:40-45, Mark 2:1-12, Luke 23:34, 40-43, Ezekiel 36:24-28, Psalm 51, and many more.

If my **desire** is to grow in **knowledge and love of Jesus**, I can choose *texts* from the gospels that carry the teachings of Jesus and *scenes* through which I observe and meet him in prayer; I learn to become like him by absorbing his teachings and especially by *letting* him meet me in prayer.

✠ Some *teaching* texts would be:
Matt 5:1-12, 43-48, Matt 13:44-46, Matt 25:31-40, Mark 4:1-20, Mark 12:41-44, Luke 6:17-36, Luke 10:25-37, Luke 12:22-34, Luke 15:11-32, John 6:35-48, John 10:11-21, John 14:1-6, John 15:1-8, 9-17.

✠ Some *scenes*:
Matt 4:1-11, Matt 14:22-33, Matt 26:36-46, Mark 4:35-41, Mark 10:46-52, Mark 14:66-72, Luke 1:26-38, Luke 2:1-20, Luke 2:41-52, Luke 19:1-10, Luke 23:32-49, John 6:1-15, John 11:17-44, John 12:1-11, John 13:1-17, John 20:10-18, 19-29, John 21:1-19.

These references are but a few samples. It would be good to explore the four gospels for other texts. This journey of growing in the intimate knowledge of Jesus is, of course, lifelong.

My prayer could arise out of **need** or out of **gratitude**. I may **desire** to meet God in prayer because I want his **help** in some difficulty, or I want his **guidance** or his **strengthening**. Many psalms could express my attitude for me and deepen my trust. Helpful psalms when in **need**: Psalms 13, 17, 23, 25, 27, 31, 43, 54, 61, 62, 70, 88, 121.

Or I may begin prayer with gratitude, a **desire** to give **thanks**, aware as I am that my gifts are from God. I name my blessings and I acknowledge the Giver. I praise God for his goodness. Many psalms will help me to express myself better and will enlarge my heart, as for example, Psalms 34, 40, 66, 68, 92, 95, 100, 103, 107, 116, 117, 124, 137.

Desire *during* prayer

✠A **second aspect of desire** is that I use it, not only as my guide in **choosing** a text, but I also use desire as my guide in how I **deal with** the text during prayer. Say, for example, that out of a **desire** to meet Jesus and know him, I am using Luke 5:1-11 — the miraculous catch of fish and the call of the first four disciples. My desire will help me during prayer to **stay focused** on meeting Jesus and avoid being side-tracked by wondering where on Lake Gennesaret the incident happened, or what was it like for Zebedee when his sons left him to follow Jesus. My **desire** to meet Jesus will help me to filter out the peripheral aspects of the scene and stay focused on Jesus. [If Zebedee's predicament does draw me, my desire will guide me to see how it connects with the cost for me of following Jesus myself.]. By being guided by my **desire** I am letting myself be **guided by the Lord** who is giving me my authentic desires.

Chapter 16
The Sign of the Cross

"Prayer begins with…"
How would you complete that sentence?

✣ Prayer begins with… a pause…or a quietening exercise… or adverting to God's presence…or lighting a candle…or a desire to give thanks…or a sense of duty…and so on. But most of us consider we start prayer with the Sign of the Cross.

The sign of the Cross is simple, comprised of a few special words and a gesture. It combines external and internal elements. We use it to start our prayers, especially when in a group, and often also to bring them to a close. It can be our way of turning towards God, and then afterwards of taking our leave. Both the gesture and the accompanying words are rich in meaning, but we use them so often that we rarely advert to their significance. We hardly notice what we are doing; we are in a hurry to begin prayer; we think that making the Sign of the Cross is not itself prayer but merely a doorway leading to prayer. We may make it with due reverence but without particular attention because we want to get on to reciting a Hail Mary or an Our Father or are beginning to celebrate Mass. Yet, as one author has said, "There are few moments of prayer that are so intense, and so concentrated in meaning as the making of the Sign of the Cross." (L. Alonso Shökel*). It is itself a prayer. The reflections that follow are an attempt to uncover some of the rich meaning of this prayer.

---

* Celebrating the Eucharist (page 9) by L. Alonso Shökel SJ. Translated from Italian in 1988. St Paul Publications, Slough, England.

A gospel scene

⧫The gospel scene that comes to mind in relation to the Sign of the Cross is Luke's account of the transfiguration of Jesus in chapter 9. Jesus has gone up the mountain to pray. The three apostles he brings with him will be witnesses also of his agony in the garden. Here now Jesus is the Son opening himself to his Father's delight in him. He lets himself be loved and is taken over so completely by the Spirit of Love that his body is transfigured; there is no resistance in him. This absence of resistance is evident also in the attitude of his heart, for he is saying an unresisting "yes" to the suffering he knows is before him, his Cross. Here in the peak of consolation he is saying a total "yes" to the reality before him: his "yes" is to the reality of human rejection because the Father wills him to go through this for our sake. We know that this "yes" is the stance of his heart because we are told he is conversing with Moses and Elijah about his "departure", his "exodus", which he predicted to the Twelve about nine days previously. He had said, "The Son of Man must undergo great suffering, and be rejected by the elders, chief priests, and scribes, and be killed, and on the third day be raised." (Lk 9:22) The Cross is part of the journey opening up before him, and here now in his heart he is saying a full "yes" to it. This "yes" is opening him here on the mountain to his Father's love. This "yes" is so pleasing to the Father that he envelops his Son in consolation; this fullness of love between them is the Spirit of Love. It is striking to note that his "yes" to the Cross brings Jesus to the peak of union with his Father. Surrender to the Cross, surrender to Love, "yes" to terrible reality.

Jesus embraces his Cross from within the depth of his place in the Trinity. Our sign of the Cross also has both dimensions, **Cross** and **Trinity**: union with the Trinity, and the following of Christ which includes embracing the cross.

Let us explore some of the meanings of our Sign of the Cross.

In the name of

✠ The words "in the name of the Father and of the Son and of the Holy Spirit" come from Mt 28:19 where Jesus commissions the Eleven Apostles. He said, "Go therefore and make disciples of all nations, baptising them in the name of the Father and of the Son and of the Holy Spirit." The words **"in the name of** the Father, Son and Holy Spirit" refer to the **effect** of baptism which is union with the Three Persons of the Trinity. This gives a clue as to their meaning. **Belonging** is expressed. The baptised person enters the loving embrace of the Three Persons, becomes attached to them, drawn into them, immersed in them, interacts with them: the words express **a new relationship**.

Two meanings

"In the name of" has two meanings.

1) It can signify that one is acting "In the name of another," that is, as a representative of someone. This is our common usage. It is found in the Bible also, as for instance, in Ex 5: 23; Deut 18:20, 22; I Sam 25:5-9; I Kings 22:16; Jer 20:9; etc.

2) But there is a second usage. This is the one which applies to the words in the baptism formula and in our Sign of the Cross. "In the name of" expresses **belonging**, dedication, consecration. An example in modern language expresses the point. When we speak of transferring the legal ownership of property to someone else, we say we are putting the property "in the name of" that person, which means into the **ownership** of that person. Similarly, when the Bible speaks of baptising someone "in the name of Jesus" or "in the name of the Trinity", the meaning is that of placing someone in the possession of Jesus or of the Trinity; it is

a consecration, a total dedication, a union, **a belonging**. It implies a surrender to Christ as Lord and Saviour, and a union with the Father, Son and Holy Spirit. It is a new relationship. (Note that the word "possession" can have negative connotations that do not apply here: for the belonging we are speaking of is the fruit of a mutual love in which personal freedom is honoured.)

"Name"

Another point needs to be made. The Bible's use of the word "name" is very different from ours. For us a name is a word we attach to a person or object. But in biblical usage the name means the *nature*, the *character*, the *personality* of the person in so far as it is known or revealed to us. You could say the name of a person is a **substitute** for the person; the name **is** the person. Yahweh is present and active when his name is invoked or called upon; to call upon his **name** is to summon **him**. Goliath approaches David with spear and javelin, but David meets him with **the name of Yahweh** (I Sam 17:45). Here the name is the calling upon the name, an utterance which makes present Yahweh himself and his power.

The **New Testament** is continuous with the Old Testament in its use of "name". Take a few examples. Simon is given a new name by Jesus, "**Peter**", meaning "rock", which is his new identity and describes his new meaning in the Church. Saul's name was changed to **Paul** when he was baptised and became a changed man in the service of Christ: Paul writes of a "new creation". Jesus works **in the name of the Father** (Jn 10:25), which here means what he says elsewhere, that he is in the Father and the Father is **in** him (Jn 14:10). He glorifies the **name** of the Father by bringing recognition of his Father's divinity (Jn 12:28). He prays that the Father will keep the disciples **in his name** (Jn 17:11), that is, that he will preserve them in himself, in his possession, be a "father" to them. In the commandment to baptise (Mt 28:19), baptism **in the name** means entry into **communion** with the Son who is united with the Father and the Holy Spirit; it is entry into the inner life of the Three Persons.

The sign

As we have seen, the **words** we use, "in the name of the Father and of the Son and of the Holy Spirit" express **belonging**, union. So also does the sign we make on ourselves. The sign is like a branding or a seal to mark **ownership**, the Lord's ownership of us in a relationship of mutual love. From earliest times, ownership was indicated by a sign, such as a signature or a seal. A seal impressed upon soft wax attested to the authenticity of a legal document or a personal letter. Gold and silver objects are known to be of genuine metal by the hallmark imprinted on them. Trademarks are used to prove the quality of an article, say of clothing. We see a circle with three spokes and we recognise the make of the car: the sign tells us that this is a genuine Mercedes and so it is a mark of quality. A sign can say so much. It is like a summary.

The sign of the Cross which we make on ourselves is like a modern logo; it is a label, a badge, a nameplate, a mark of **identification**. It marks in a summary way who we are and, even more, **whose** we are. It is a sign of our **belonging to Christ**.

Baptism

The mark of the cross was first traced on us during our baptism when the priest said: "N., the Christian community welcomes you with great joy. In its name I **claim** you for Christ our Saviour by the sign of the cross. I now trace the sign of the cross on your forehead, and invite your parents and godparents to do the same."

This sign, which we now make on ourselves, is a sign of

our consecration to the Lord, our attachment to him. By it we acknowledge the Lord's **claim** on us. By it, I am saying, "I am the Lord's" (Is. 44:5), and by it the Lord is saying to me, "You are mine" (Is 43:1)

Belonging

In the **Song of Songs**, the bride says passionately, "Set me as a seal upon your heart, as a seal upon your arm" (8:6).She wishes to belong totally and irrevocably to the other. "Set me as a seal upon your heart," so that I may be completely yours. Elsewhere in the **Song** she phrased it differently: "My Beloved is mine and I am his."(Song 2:16; 6:3; 7:10)

Our Sign of the Cross, even without the words which call on the Trinity, is saying the same: "I belong to Christ: I am his and he is mine." Christ's sign, the cross first traced on us at baptism, has marked us as **belonging** to him in a relationship of mutual love. Each time I sign myself with the Cross, I remind myself of the love unto death by which Christ earned his claim on me, and here I now surrender to him.

The Cross

Our belonging to Christ is our dignity, but it also carries a **responsibility**. The sign we trace on ourselves represents a **challenge** to take up our own cross every day, and even to **desire** the cross for the sake of Christ who has made us his own in baptism. We are to "take it up", for it is there already in the irksome inconveniences of daily life. (Lk 9:23) We are to face into it, say "yes" to it, want it to be there, for the cross is one of those places where Christ is **waiting** for us. Unless we engage with our cross and meet Jesus there, we will find ourselves at some distance from the place where he is receiving the delight of his Father in him: we will be in the wrong place. We won't be open enough to hear the Father say to us also in some way, "You are my daughter, my son, whom I love; in you I delight." (Lk 3:22) We won't be able to taste properly who we are, the **desired** of the Father and of the Son and of the Holy Spirit.

Praying the Sign of the Cross: some images

✠ A few images or metaphors may help us to pray the Sign of the Cross.

A doorway

We start prayer with the Sign of the Cross, so you could see it as a **doorway** of prayer. I stand in this doorway reminding myself that God is one and also three, three Persons in one God, for we say 'in the name', not 'in the names'. It is an **act of faith**. I am accepting God's revelation of himself which I learned through Jesus Christ, and so I **salute** my God by naming the Father and the Son and the Holy Spirit.

A foundation stone

In this doorway, I pause and stand a moment. I stand here as a child of the Father, an enormous claim, and an amazing dignity. I do not deserve this; I have not earned it; it is sheer gift, bestowed at my baptism. I am standing here in the shoes, so to speak, of Jesus the Son and am being gazed upon by his Father. This **ground** on which I stand is the *starting place* of all Christian prayer, the **foundation stone** of prayer. I belong here; this space is home. Yet I am here by invitation. I dare to believe that the word which the Father spoke to Jesus at his baptism is being addressed also now to me: "You are my daughter, my son, whom I love; in you I delight." (Lk 3:22)

An embrace

Here I am in the **embrace** of the Three Persons, the invisible embrace of my God. I am in the space that belongs to the Son; with him I am under the loving gaze of the Father; I am included in the interplay of love that is going on between the Father and the Son. I may not have experience of it yet, but this is what God began to share with me at baptism. The Spirit is at work drawing me further in.

A thurible

Our sign of the Cross is not only a doorway, a salutation, and act of faith, an embrace, but it is also like the swing of a **thurible** by which I honour my God and hold myself in worship before One who is awesome, yet intimate.

A veil

By the sign of the Cross at the beginning of prayer I draw aside a veil, as it were, from my eyes to look with eyes of faith at the God who has unveiled himself to me through his incarnate Son. The Sign of the Cross is the answer to my question, "How is God looking at me?" God is looking at me as his child, I am beholding my Father; in me he sees Jesus; by the action of his Spirit he is delighting in me; I surrender to this love. I am not searching for God: God has found me, and I advert to this.

An inner lift

By the sign of the Cross I go down an **inner lift** to the room of my heart; I wait for the door on the past and the future to be shut; and now in this present moment I find my Father waiting for me. (Mt 6:6) Here, too, is Jesus; and his Spirit is enabling me to be present to them both. This is true even if I am not able to have experience of it.

Membership card

I belong here in this Trinitarian space. This is home. I have been given a place in this divine community. The Sign of the Cross is **my membership card.**

A Summary

Cross Sign: I am yours, Jesus...I accept your way...I say "yes" to daily dying to my ego-self...I find you there.

In the name: Belonging ..Embraced ..Immersed ..Consecrated ..Situated in...Within.

Of the Father: Gazing on me, his daughter/son..."I delight in you" .. Draw me deeper.

And of the Son: I am in your space, Jesus...I want to be like you...I am yours...With you I take up my cross...I receive the Father's love in you.

And of the Holy Spirit: Spirit, you connect me to the Father and the Son...I am enabled by you...I want to surrender to your action in me.

✠ Cross sign ...."I am yours, Jesus,

In the name ....Embraced,

of the Father ....by the Father, gazing on me,

and of the Son ....in your space of Sonship, Jesus,

and of the Holy Spirit ....surrendered to your Spirit"

Amen ....Amen.

Chapter 17

Conclusion

✤Prayer is a journey. Dag Hammarskjold wrote in *Markings* (page 65), "The longest journey is the journey inward." Personal prayer is part of that journey, even intrinsic to it when you consider that the ultimate journey is one of recognising God with our heart and of letting him take over our heart: he wants union. Through prayer, we grow in our perception of who God truly is, and we discover with some embarrassment that our response to his love is often self-centred. God is offering us a conscious relationship in faith with himself, with a longing for us beyond our comprehension or deserts. We learn how to meet with God, bringing our real self and its mixture into his welcoming presence, and opening ourselves to his loving gaze. We ask to have our focus right in our life and our prayer; we ask to want God for himself, and to surrender to his loving will. The Spirit is at work in us connecting us with Jesus and the Father, and enabling us to grow into our share of the space Jesus has before the Father. Imagination helps us to meet with the Jesus of the gospels, who reveals the Father, and to receive his compassion and healing and open ourselves to intimacy with him. Jesus leads us to the Father, who is the Mysterious One who encompasses all the qualities of a mother and a father, and is the desire of our hearts. Our desiring is complex, but the Lord can sift it and cure it until we are graced with a love which is largely without self-interest.

In the end, we may find, like St Paul, that Jesus lives in us, so that we love with his love, pray with the prayer he gives us, forgive with his forgiving heart, are patient with his patience, and we carry our cross alongside him and meet with him there. This is where he wants to bring us: it is the flowering of the grace of our baptism. In the final analysis, our prayer and our holiness are, of course, God's work in us. All is gift.

Closing prayer:

Father, let the gift of your life continue to grow in us,
*drawing us **from** death **to** faith, hope and love.*
Keep us alive in Christ Jesus.
Keep us watchful in prayer and true to his teaching
till your glory is revealed in us.
We ask this through Christ Our Lord. Amen.

[Missal, 16th Sunday]

Appendix for Retreatants

✤These chapters originally had retreatants in mind, specifically those making a directed retreat of 8 full days. Two issues arise for retreatants as their retreat is drawing to a close: (1) how to regard the last two days of the retreat so as to get the most from them; and (2) how to review the retreat as a whole so as to gather the fruit of it. An appendix to cover these two topics may be of help.

Part One: As a Retreat Is Ending

✤On a retreat of 8 full days, the deepest days are likely to be days 4, 5 and 6. On days 1 to 3, I disposed myself for reaching this depth. I drew aside from the usual preoccupations and responsibilities of my day-to-day life. I opened myself to God's action during prayer. Now I have slowed down and am more present to myself and to the present moment. Day 8 and the future seem far away. I have the feeling of being in a timeless zone. By drawing back from conversation and from busyness, I have created a certain solitude *around* myself and have entered a zone of solitude *inside* myself where I have become sensitive to the "gentle, whispering sound" of the Lord's voice. (1 Kings 19:12) This depth of quiet and this sensitivity and availability to God are the fruit of my willingness to be alone and of my receiving the action of God in successive times of prayer. I can appreciate these words of Brother Roger of Taizé: "In everyone there is a zone of solitude that no human intimacy can fill: it is there that God encounters us...Here, in the hollow of our being, we discover the Risen Christ." (*Festival Without End*, p.15) St Ignatius puts it this way in the *Spiritual Exercises* with a wisdom born of experience:

"The more we keep ourselves alone and secluded, the more fit do we make ourselves to approach and attain our Creator and Lord: and the more we unite ourselves to him in this way, the more do we dispose ourselves to receive graces and gifts from his divine and supreme goodness."

(Sp Ex #20)

During those deep days, I have received the closeness of the Risen Christ in my heart. I know something of the supreme goodness of my Lord in the hollow of my being.

Day Seven

But now this is Day 7, and the time after the retreat is beginning to intrude. I am surfacing; this is natural and inevitable. The future is coming into the present. But I am not entirely at the mercy of the future. I have a choice of attitude before me. There are two ways of looking at days 7 and 8: (1) I can look on days 7 and 8 as the days before my exit from my retreat; in this way I can allow the future to encroach upon my attention more and more. (2) Or, on the other hand, I can regard days 7 and 8 as days that I have spent 6 other days building up to. In this way, I can hold 7 and 8 as precious, and I can choose to guard the precious solitude of heart that has developed in me. I can view those two days as ones on which to hold myself gentle and quiet, keeping myself in the present moment so as to be available to "the still, small voice" of the Lord, whose voice is like "the sound of sheer silence." (I Kings 19:12) The Lord's voice comes as "a light, murmuring sound", and now, on the final two days, he is waiting to bestow gifts upon me.

What if I didn't create a solitude?

But maybe I didn't build a space around myself so as to

be truly alone with God. Perhaps I was afraid to take a chance on staying apart from my mobile phone. Maybe I was afraid of what might come up for me. Could it be that I was using reading as an escape from facing myself and my inner poverty and my need of God? It is dawning on me now that I was holding myself back from God by staying on the surface of myself. I am beginning to feel disappointed with myself. With thoughts like these, I could be tempted to immerse myself in regrets.

I suggest, instead, a creative way of looking at the situation: it is not too late to face up to reality. Maybe I am ready now, after 6 days of retreat, such as they were, to make a gesture of generosity and trust towards the Lord that will open me and dispose me to receive gifts from the Lord, who is still longing to be generous to me in ways that I do not expect. I suggest that it is not too late even now to make the most of days 7 and 8. How will I do this? By drawing back now to be more alone with the Lord; by being more earnest about prayer; by bringing my sorrow to the Lord and by trusting that I am still loved as I am. Do I believe that he still wants to be generous to me? Will I hold myself receptive before "his divine and supreme goodness", as St Ignatius invites?

Closing Prayer:

> Grant, O Lord, that your love may
> so fill our lives that we may count
> nothing too small to do for you,
> nothing too much to give, and
> nothing too hard to bear
> for Jesus' sake. Amen.

Part Two: Gathering The Fruit

✚ On the final retreat day, time could usefully be spent looking back over what happened so as to take full advantage of it: I am talking about follow-through.

Jesus, in John 6:12, after feeding the 5,000 with the five loaves and two fish, told the apostles, "Gather the pieces left over. Let nothing be wasted."

"Let nothing be wasted," he said. It is indeed possible to let an 8-day retreat get wasted. People sometimes wonder why the annual retreat has produced little or no effect. What does it profit a person to spend 8 days on retreat if no change or development seems to have come from it? What do I need to do so as to ensure that my investment of 8 days is going to produce a good dividend for me?

What message? What gift?

I suggest that it could be good for us, on the final day of the retreat, to look over what happened during the retreat and to pick up on what the Lord has been saying to me. I might ask myself what was God's message to me that I am to take away from this retreat and work on until the next annual retreat. God's programme for me for the coming year may well have been indicated to me. What has God been teaching me? What change has happened in me that I am called to work at integrating into my everyday life?

The first thing to do is to name God's message and gift, so that I can then hold on to it and work with it. I could, perhaps, take these two broad headings: change in prayer, and change in attitude.

Change in prayer

How has my praying been? What change do I see?

1) Perhaps I have been brought to a new stage in which

less material is enough now to hold me in the presence of God. What does this say? Does it tell me that I have been using too much material for prayer and am now being asked to settle for what quietens me and holds me in loving attention to God? Less now is more. Am I to go deep now by revisiting, in successive times of prayer, material that has engaged me, and let go of my old practice of covering fresh material each time I pray?

2) Perhaps in prayer I have been brought below words and images and ideas, and am now in a prayer of attitude, a prayer of faith, where texts don't help during full prayer. My prayer is more a be-ing than a do-ing. It is an attitude, say, of trust or of surrender or of desiring or of waiting or of listening, like picking up a distant sound at the edge of hearing. It may seem poor, for it is harder to report on, but it is the way God wants me to be now when I come to pray, and it is actually deeper. Will I continue to pray as God wants me to pray?

3) Perhaps I have faced up to my neglect of enough formal personal prayer in my daily life, and am called now to put God really in the first place. Do I know what to do in order to follow through on this realisation?

4) Perhaps my real discovery in this retreat is that prayer is a relationship, not a task or an achievement, and that I am being asked now to share control in prayer by listening and waiting. What image of prayer with help me to stay with this insight? Maybe to see prayer as a meeting, or to see that Someone important is waiting for me, or maybe letting the Lord look at me lovingly and humbly, as St Teresa of Jesus suggested. Or it may be that I have discovered how necessary it is for me to become present to myself first at the start of prayer by asking myself, "How am I just now?"

Looking at attitude

Besides looking back at my way of praying, I could also look at the content of my praying and see if I was brought into a change of attitude that I have to work on and integrate.

1) Perhaps a healing of memories has happened for me through prayer. Do I now have to really let go of that part of my past, and trust what the Lord was saying and doing in me? Resist the temptation to return to the hurt and anger and the negative self-image?

2) Did I discover the attitude towards the past or towards the future that allayed my anxiety and brought peace, and enabled me to be in the present moment much more than ever before? Will I work with this? Will I stay with this new attitude?

3) Perhaps in prayer I was led to accepting myself as I am, imperfect, a work-in-progress, a sinner and yet loved undeservedly. Have I to work now at really accepting this message, and move away from self-preoccupation?

4) Did I discover an attitude to somebody in my life which I know is a Christlike attitude and is what the Risen Lord wants me now to live and to continue?

Old habits versus the new

As I said at the beginning of my suggestions, the first thing to do is to name the message, this gift. The second thing to do is to face a certain reality. We know this reality already from our previous retreats. It is this.

I have seen something new, and I have experienced something new during these 8 days. And what is new has brought me consolation and a certain sense of freedom. I may even feel that I am a new person. But the old habits have been in me for much longer that 8 days; they are very well in place. They won't be shifted by an experience of 8 days unless I keep the new thing consciously before my mind, and keep working to integrate the gift that has been given to me. I must follow through. I have to develop a new habit which will displace the old habit. Part of me will be resisting this change, and that makes perfect sense; I must expect this resistance to the new.

But there are two energies on my side in favour of the new development. First of all, my psyche has a drive for health and wholeness. And secondly, the Holy Spirit is an energy in me to move me forward; the Holy Spirit is on my side enabling me to integrate the new gift that the Lord has revealed in me.

What plan?

Lastly, how will I stay aware of the Lord's message and gift during the coming year? What plan will I form? Perhaps I could set aside a day or part of a day once a month for an extended time of reflection and prayer. Or better still, I could incorporate the message of the retreat into the Examen of Consciousness which I use every evening to go back over my day to see how God was present and acting there, and how I responded. In addition, lest I rely too much on my own resolve only, I could share my plan with a friend or a spiritual director who will encourage me to keep to it.

The Lord Jesus said, "Gather the pieces left over. Let nothing be wasted." (John 6:12)

Closing Prayer:

Dear Jesus, help me to spread your fragrance
everywhere I go.
Flood my soul with your spirit and life.
Penetrate and possess my being so utterly
that all my life may be only a radiance of yours.
Shine through me and be so in me
that every soul I come in contact with
may feel your presence in my soul.
Let them look up and see
no longer me but only you, O Lord.

[Blessed John Henry Newman]

Summary
The Steps of Approach to Prayer

✠ *Step One:* Presence to self: "How am I?"

✠ *Step Two:* Presence to God:
I look towards God:
"Where am I going, and for what purpose?"
I enter God's gaze:
"How is God looking at me?"

✠ *Step Three:* I ask for the grace to get my basic
focus right – to serve and praise God.

✠ *Step Four:* I use my imagination: I compose a picture
so as to compose myself.

✠ *Step Five:* I focus my desire and I ask God for
what I want.

✠ *Step Six:* • I move *from* reflecting *to* relating.
• I close with an Our Father.